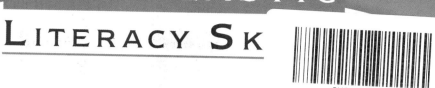

Comprehension
Year 5

TERMS AND CONDITIONS

IMPORTANT – PERMITTED USE AND WARNINGS – READ CAREFULLY BEFORE USING

Minimum system requirements:

- PC or Mac with CD-ROM drive (16x speed recommended) and 512MB RAM
- P4 or G4 processor
- Windows 2000/XP/Vista or Mac OS 10.3 to 10.6

For all technical support queries, please phone Scholastic Customer Services on 0845 6039091.

Author

Donna Thomson and
Elspeth Graham

Editor

Rachel Mackinnon

Assistant editors

Gaynor Spry, Suzanne Adams and
Vicky Butt

**CD-ROM design and
development team**

Joy Monkhouse, Anna Oliwa,
Micky Pledge, Rebecca Male, Allison Parry,
Q&D Multimedia and Haremi

Series designers

Shelley Best and Anna Oliwa

Book layout

Quadrum Solutions Ltd

Illustrations

JHS Studio/Beehive Illustration

Designed using Adobe Indesign
Published by Scholastic Ltd,
Book End, Range Road, Witney,
Oxfordshire OX29 0YD
www.scholastic.co.uk

Printed by Bell & Bain Ltd, Glasgow
Text © 2009 Donna Thomson and Elspeth Graham
© 2009 Scholastic Ltd
10 11 12 13 14 15 16 17 18 19   4 5 6 7 8

British Library Cataloguing-in-Publication Data
A catalogue record for this book is available from
the British Library.
ISBN 978-1407-10053-1

Acknowledgements

The publishers gratefully acknowledge permission to reproduce the following
copyright material: **BBC** for the use of the leaflet 'Give a bird a home' © 2007, BBC
(2007, www.bbc.co.uk/breathingplaces). **Nick Butterworth** for the electronic use
of an extract from *Making Faces* by Nick Butterworth © 1993, Nick Butterworth
(1993, Walker Books). **Curtis Brown Group Ltd** for the electronic use of an
extract from *Carrie's War* by Nina Bawden © 1973, Nina Bawden (1973, Puffin).
Dorling Kindersely for the use of images from *Children's Quick & Easy Cookbook*
by Angela Wilkes © 1997, Dorling Kindersley (1997, Dorling Kindersley). **John
Foster** for the use of 'Facts about air' by John Foster from *Standing on the sidelines*
by John Foster © 1995, John Foster (1995, Oxford University Press). **Kids Can
Press** for the use of the poem 'Pearls' by Jean Little from *Hey World, Here I am!*
by Jean Little © 1986, Jean Little (1986, Kids Can Press). **Christopher Leach** for
the use of 'Blackbird' by Christopher Leach © Christopher Leach. **Macmillan
Children's Books** for the use of an extract from *Millions* by Frank Cottrell Boyce
© 2004, Frank Cottrell Boyce (2004, Macmillan Children's Books) and for the use
of an extract from *The Black Book of Secrets* by F E Higgins © 2007, F E Higgins
(2007, Macmillan Children's Books). **Sarah Matthews** for the use of the poem
'Chips' by Stanley Cook from *A Second Poetry Book* compiled by John Foster
© 1980, The Estate of Stanley Cook (1980, Oxford University Press). **Oxford
University Press** for the use of an extract from *The Turbulent Term of Tyke
Tiler* by Gene Kemp © 2003, Gene Kemp (2003, Oxford Playscripts). **Penguin
Group UK** for the use of an extract from *Carrie's War* by Nina Bawden © 1973,
Nina Bawden (1973, Puffin) and for the use of an extract from "Children's Quick
and Easy Cookbook" by Angela Wilkes © 1997, Angela Wilkes (1997, Dorling
Kindersley). **Random House Group** for the print use of text and illustration from
Falling Angels by Colin Thompson © 2001, Colin Thompson (2001, Hutchinson)
and for the use of text and illustrations from *Ethel and Ernest* by Raymond Briggs
© 1998, Raymond Briggs (1998, Jonanthan Cape). **Rogers, Coleridge & White
Ltd** for the electronic use of an extract from *Falling Angels* by Colin Thompson
© 2001, Colin Thompson (2001, Hutchinson). **Scholastic Children's Books** for
the use of an extract from *Ways to live forever* by Sally Nicholls © 2008, Sally
Nicholls (2008, Scholastic). **Simon & Schuster** for the use of an extract from
Exchange by Paul Magrs © 2006, Paul Magrs (2006, Simon & Schuster) and for
the use of the cover of *Tales of Mystery and Madness* by Edgar Allan Poem,
illustrated by Gris Grimly © 2004, Gris Grimly (2004, Simon & Schuster). **Walker
Books** for an illustration from *Alice's adventures in Wonderland* by Lewis Carroll
and illustrated by Helen Oxenbury, illustration © 1999, Helen Oxenbury (1999,
Walker Books); for text and illustrations from *Pirate Diary* by Richard Platt and
illustrated by Chris Riddell, text © 2001, Richard Platt, illustration © 2001, Chris
Riddell (2001, Walker Books); text and illustration from *Peter and the Wolf* by
Selina Hastings and illustrated by Reg Cartwright, text © 1987, Selina Hastings,
illustration © 1987, Reg Cartwright (1987, Walker Books); text and illustrations
from *When Jessie Came Across the Sea* by Amy Hest, text © 1997, Amy Hest,
illustrations © 1997, P J Lynch (1997, Walker Books); for the print use of text and
illustrations from *Making Faces* by Nick Butterworth © 1993, Nick Butterworth
(1993, Walker Books); for the use of text and an illustration from *Castle Diary*
by Richard Platt, text © 1999, Richard Platt, illustration © 1999, Chris Riddell
(1999, Walker Books); for the use of the cover of *Keeper* by Mal Peet, cover
illustration © 2006, Phil Schramm and for the use of text and illustrations from
Chaucers Canterbury Tales retold and illustrated by Marcia Williams © 2007,
Marcia Williams (2007, Walker Books). **Walker Books** for the use of an extract
from *Stormbreaker™ – The Graphic Novel* based on the screenplay by Anthony
Horowitz; adapted by Antony Johnson; illustrated by Kanako and Yuzuru. Text
and illustration © 2006, Walker Books Ltd. Screenplay © MMVI Samuelson/IoM
Film. Film © MMVI Film & Entertainment VIP Medienfolds 4 GmbH & Co. KG.
Style Guide © MMVI ARR Ltd. Trademarks 2006 Samuelson Productions Ltd.
Stormbreaker™ Alex Rider™. Reproduced by permission of Walker Books Ltd.

Contents

Chapter 1
Retelling

Chapter 2
Literal questioning

Chapter 3
Prediction

Chapter 4
Inference

Chapter 5
Clarification

Chapter 6
Evaluation

Chapter 7
Review

Introduction

The Scholastic Literacy Skills: Comprehension series

Comprehension is the ability to understand and elicit meaning from any type of written or illustrated material. It is the reason for reading. If readers can read the words but do not understand what they mean, they are not really reading.

This series offers teachers carefully structured guidance on how to use the essential comprehension skills of summarising, predicting, clarifying and questioning to extract the author's meaning. Each book is progressive and supports the teaching and development of these comprehension strategies. The series also offers teachers a generic framework for teaching reciprocal reading – a process that provides children with the confidence to explore and enjoy a range of 'real' books beyond the samples featured in the series. The skills pages show the children how to gather information, respond to questions meaningfully and generate their own literal, inferential and evaluative questions from quality fiction and non-fiction extracts. It also provides levelled comprehension assessment materials that correlate with NC reading age levels.

Overview of the teaching of comprehension

To fully engage children in the reading process and help them to explore and make sense of a range of text, they need to understand the skills involved in how we make meaning. Alongside summarising, clarifying and predicting, they need to be able to identify and apply the three fundamental questioning skills:

- Literal – explicit meaning. (Who? What? Where?)
- Inference – hidden and implied meaning. (Detective work – thinking and searching for clues to make deductions. Why? How do you know that?)
- Evaluation – personal meaning. (Using own experience to explain events or characters' actions, feelings and behaviour and linking them to the author's viewpoint. Why do you think…?)

These skills enable children to have full understanding of information, whether it is presented through text or pictures and are central to bringing meaning and reasoning to learning to read and learning in general.

Comprehension is not something that happens after reading. Good readers use their experience and

knowledge of the world, alongside their knowledge of vocabulary and language structure, to make sense of the text and relate to the author's viewpoint. Good readers monitor their understanding as they read and know how to resolve their difficulties with comprehension as the problems arise.

About the product

This book contains seven chapters. Each chapter focuses on a different aspect of comprehension, and is organised into four sections with clear objectives, background information, teaching ideas and photocopiable pages for use in whole-class teaching, with groups or for independent work. Each chapter also features a poster.

Posters

Each chapter has one poster which relates to the subject of the chapter. It should be displayed and used for reference throughout the work on the chapter. The poster notes (on the chapter opening page) offer suggestions for how they could be used. There is a black and white version in the book and full-colour version on the CD-ROM for you to print or display on a whiteboard.

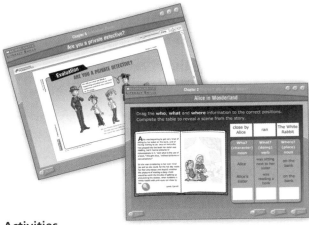

Activities

Each section contains two activities. These activities all take the form of a photocopiable page which is in the book and on the CD-ROM for you to display or print out (these pages are also provides with answers where appropriate). Over thirty of the photocopiable pages have linked interactive activities on the CD-ROM. These interactive activities are designed to act as starter activities to the lesson, giving whole-class support on the information being taught. However, they can also work equally well as plenary activities, reviewing the work the children have just completed.

Using the CD-ROM

Below are brief guidance notes for using the CD-ROM. For more detailed information, see **How to use** on the start-up screen, or **Help** on the relevant screen for information about that page.

The CD-ROM follows the structure of the book and contains:

- All of the photocopiable pages, with answers where appropriate.
- All of the poster pages in full colour.
- Over thirty interactive on-screen activities linked to the photocopiable pages.

Getting started

To begin using the CD-ROM, simply place it in your CD- or DVD-ROM drive. Although the CD-ROM should auto-run, if it fails to do so, navigate to the drive and double-click on the red **Start** icon.

Start-up screen

This is the first screen where you can access: terms and conditions, registration link, how to use the CD-ROM and credits. If you agree to the terms and conditions, click **Start** to continue.

Main menu

Clicking on the relevant **Chapter** icon will take you to the chapter screen where you can access the posters and the chapter's sections. Clicking on **All resources** will take you to a list of all the resources, where you can search by key word or a specific resource.

Section screen

Upon choosing a section from the chapter screen, you are taken to a list of resources for that section. Here you can access all of the photocopiable pages and interactive activities linked to that section.

Resource finder

This lists all of the resources on the CD-ROM. You can:

- Select a chapter and/or section by selecting the appropriate title from the drop-down menus.
- Search for key words.
- Scroll through the list of resources.
- Launch a resource by clicking once on its row.

Navigation

The resources (poster pages, photocopiable pages and interactive activities) all open in separate windows on top of the menu screen. To close a resource, click on the **x** in the top right-hand corner. To return to the menu screen you can either close or minimise a resource.

Closing a resource will not close the program. However, if you are in a menu screen, then clicking on the **x** will close the program. To return to a previous menu screen, you need to click on the **Back** button.

Whiteboard tools

The CD-ROM comes with its own set of whiteboard tools for use on any whiteboard.
These include:

- Pen tool
- Highlighter tool
- Eraser
- Sticky note

Click on the **Tools** button at the foot of the screen to access these tools.

Printing

Print the resources by clicking on the **Print** button. The photocopiable pages print as A4 portrait pages, but please note that a landscape poster or photocopiable page needs the orientation set to landscape in your print preferences. The interactive activities will print what is on the screen. For a full A4 printout you need to set the orientation to landscape in your print preferences.

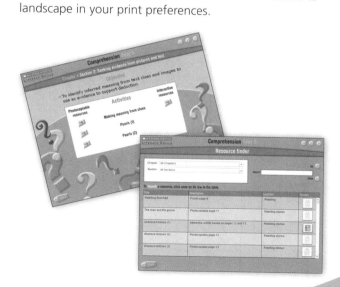

Framework objectives

Page		Section	Literacy skills objective	Strand 7: Make notes on and use evidence from across a text to explain events or ideas.	Strand 7: Infer writers' perspectives from what is written and from what is implied.	Strand 7: Explore how writers use language for comic and dramatic effect.	Strand 8: Compare the usefulness of techniques such as visualisation, prediction and empathy in exploring the meaning of texts.
10	Chapter 1	Retelling stories	To retell, using key questions to highlight the main points at the beginning of a story.	✓			✓
14		Problem and resolution	To retell, extending the main theme and 'who', 'what' and 'where' points of non-fiction information to include the problem and how the problem is solved (resolution).	✓			✓
18		Retelling instructions	To organise non-fiction information and to retell it accurately in the correct order.	✓			
22		Sequencing	To organise story information and to retell it in sequence.	✓	✓		
28	Chapter 2	Who? What? Where?	To identify literal information about characters within pictures and text. To gather, organise and classify this information to ask and answer questions.	✓	✓		
32		Literal questions	To identify and classify literal key word information about characters, action and place within text. To respond to questions and formulate questions from text.	✓	✓		
36		Answering literal questions	To identify literal key words in the question and locate the same word(s) in the text and link them to the picture to find the answer.	✓	✓		
40		Skimming and scanning for literal meaning	To answer literal questions from text by skimming and scanning to locate the same words as the key words that appear in the question.	✓		✓	
46	Chapter 3	Cause and effect	To find clues from images and words that suggest what might happen next.	✓			
50		Anticipating before and after	To look for clues in text that suggest what may have happened before and what might happen next.	✓			✓
54		Clues from the cover	To be able to link visual clues, key words in the title and genre to make predictions.	✓			✓
58		Predicting meaning from symbolic images	Making sense of symbolic picture clues to predict purpose, meaning and possible outcomes.	✓			✓
64	Chapter 4	Inferred non-fiction clues	To identify and interpret inferred meaning from picture and text clues to better understand the author's meaning, and answer inference questions.	✓	✓		
68		Seeking evidence from pictures and text	To identify inferred meaning from text clues and images to use as evidence to support deduction.	✓	✓		
72		Presenting evidence	To gather and present evidence that indicates a full understanding of the author's intention.	✓	✓		
76		Inference questions	To gather, organise and classify inferred information to formulate questions and answers from text.	✓	✓		

Framework objectives

	Page	Section	Literacy skills objective	Strand 7: Make notes on and use evidence from across a text to explain events or ideas.	Strand 7: Infer writers' perspectives from what is written and from what is implied.	Strand 7: Explore how writers use language for comic and dramatic effect.	Strand 8: Compare the usefulness of techniques such as visualisation, prediction and empathy in exploring the meaning of texts.
Chapter 5	82	Understanding time in storytelling	To understand how authors use interchanging time sequences to tell a story.				✓
	86	Unfamiliar words	To make sense of unfamiliar words and expressions, using contextual clues and prior knowledge to seek meaning.			✓	
	90	Similes and metaphors	To be able to identify and understand metaphor within text.			✓	
	94	Skimming and scanning for similar and opposite meanings	To learn how to skim and scan for similar and opposite meanings within text and pictures that link to question key clues. To infer from these clues to answer questions and support deduction.			✓	
Chapter 6	100	Characters' feelings and actions	To draw on own experience to interpret characters' emotions and actions within pictures and text to explain what is happening or may happen next.	✓	✓	✓	
	104	What you think and feel	To understand that an evaluation question asks you to use your literal and inference skills, as well as personal experience, to think about a character's feelings or actions.	✓			
	108	Fact, opinion and evaluation	To distinguish between literal facts and personal opinion from words and images to support understanding of evaluation within non-fiction.	✓	✓		✓
	112	Evaluation questions	To understand that evaluation questions ask you to use a mix of literal, inferred and personal understanding to answer them and to generate questions about characters' feelings or actions.	✓			✓
Chapter 7	118	Non-fiction	To identify the plot and sequence of events within picture stories and to gather clues and information from non-fiction pictures and text to answer questions.	✓	✓	✓	✓
	123	Fiction	To skim and scan for literal, inferential and evaluative information. To respond to questions by locating the same, similar or opposite meanings to key words in the questions and generate questions.	✓		✓	✓

Chapter 1

Retelling

Introduction

Children's fiction and non-fiction reading comprehension improves significantly when they are shown how to retell and summarise coherently, are given the opportunity to practise often and to listen regularly to others using this skill.

When children retell and summarise it also provides teachers with an effective means of monitoring their class' real understanding of a text. This is because these skills require them to focus on the specific elements of story structure to be able to present a clear summary in logical sequence and in their own words.

Poster notes

Retelling flowchart (page 9)

A story flowchart is a useful way to support children's retelling. It offers a simple guide summarising beginning, middle and end that helps them to unravel text, focus on the main points and sequence the events within the story narrative. It helps them to:
- concentrate on the theme of the story
- classify the 'who', 'what' and 'where' information in relation to character, action and place
- establish what the problem is for the characters in the middle
- include what happens in the end to give a full summary.

In this chapter

	About the section	About the comprehension activity
Retelling stories page 10	Children look at pictures and text to establish who is in the story, what they are doing and where they are.	Children answer literal questions from a series of frames from a graphic Sherlock Holmes novel.
Problem and resolution page 14	Children begin to think about problem and resolution within stories.	Children look at a non-fiction passage about acne and infer meaning from it.
Retelling instructions page 18	Children consider the importance of sequence by looking at instructions.	Children look at instructions for 'Simon says' and answer questions about it that focus on sequencing.
Sequencing page 22	Children look at beginning, middle and end and think about the structure of stories and narrative poems.	Children look at the narrative poem 'Blackbird' by Christopher Leach and answer questions about its structure.

Retelling

Retelling flowchart

Theme – main idea

Beginning – who, what and where

Middle – problem

End – solution

Beginning
Theme – main idea of story/what it revolves around.
Who? – main story characters – **Person.**
What? – what the characters are doing – **Action.**
Where? – where the story takes place – **Place.**

Middle
Problem/conflict – what the main characters want to happen.
Events – how the characters try to solve the problem.

End
Resolution/conclusion – Is the problem solved or not solved? How did the story end? How did the main character feel?

Illustrations © 2009, JHS Studio/Beehive Illustration.

Retelling stories

Objective

To retell, using key questions to highlight the main points at the beginning of a story.

Background knowledge

When children are retelling a story it is helpful for them to remember to first refer to the overall theme (the subject matter or moral of the story) – for example, *This story is about a lost brother and sister who are held captive by a wicked witch*. The children then need to ask themselves literal questions about the pictures and text to present the main points to their audience: *Who is in the story? What are they doing? What is happening? Where are they?* From this basic information the story summary is able to unfold to include the problem and events leading to the resolution and end. These main points can provide a useful first statement to begin the story retelling. For example: *One day* (Who?) *Hansel and Gretel* (What?) *spotted a beautiful cottage made of sweets* (Where?) *in the wood*.

Skills

Explain that the activities will help the children to practise gathering the most important points from text and pictures to retell the beginning of a story in three easy steps.

● **Photocopiable page 11 'The man and the goose'**
  ● Explain that to retell, you need only repeat the main points in a story: the story theme; 'who', 'what' and 'where' information; problem and resolution. Tell the children that they are first going to practise retelling the main points of a story.

● Hand out the photocopiable sheet and ask the children to read it in pairs and discuss what is happening at the beginning of the story. Then write the sentence *A man was carrying a goose down a city street in the snow* on the board. Discuss what it says and ask them to draw a picture of the scene.

● Ask them to think carefully about the information within their picture that shows the character ('man'), his action ('carrying') and the place ('city street in the snow'). Explain that if they have included these three elements then they have picked out the main points of the sentence that tells the story.

● Ask the children to discuss the character, action and place in the other picture and underline the 'who', 'what' and 'where' information in the text.

● Finally, ask the children in pairs to practise retelling the main points of the story using the underlined information.

Comprehension

● **Photocopiable pages 12 and 13 'Sherlock Holmes'**
  ● Hand out the photocopiable sheets. Ask the children to read the text and look at the pictures.
  ● Explain to the children that they need to answer the questions about the text and pictures in full, and then ask and answer their own 'who', 'what' or 'where' question.

What's on the CD-ROM

On the CD-ROM you will find:
● Printable versions of all three photocopiable pages.
● Answers to 'Sherlock Holmes (2)'.
● Interactive version of 'Sherlock Holmes'.

Retelling stories

The man and the goose

■ What is happening in these scenes? Consider **who**, **what** and **where**.

At 4pm on Christmas Eve PC Paterson noticed a man carrying a large white goose.

As the policeman was watching him, a group of thugs walked up the street.

Simon says (2)

1. What is the main theme of the game?

_____

_____

_____

2. What do the players need to do right at the beginning of the game?

_____

_____

_____

3. Explain when the players must not move.

_____

_____

_____

4. What happens after Simon has caught out the last player?

_____

_____

_____

5. Your question:

_____

_____

Your answer:

_____

_____

Sequencing

(see poster page 9 'Retelling flowchart')

Objective

To organise story information and to retell it in sequence.

Background knowledge

Narrative poems are poems that tell stories. Like stories, they involve a sequence of events that have a beginning (which introduces the background to the story), a middle (which talks about the action of the event(s) or conflict), and an end (which resolves the event(s) and concludes the story). It is useful for children to have a scaffold to retell the sequence of these events in the correct order (see poster page 9 'Retelling flowchart').

To retell the main points of a story meaningfully, it is helpful for the children to have a sequencing guide that will help them to order their thoughts. For example:
● **Beginning:** The story is about… (Who? What? Where?)
● **Middle:** The problem is that… What happens is… the characters feel…
● **End:** What happens in the end is…

Skills

These activities give children practice in retelling the beginning, middle and end of a story in the right sequence of events.
● **Photocopiable page 23 'The Echoing Green'**
  ● Hand out the photocopiable sheet and ask the children to look at the pictures and text from left to right. Can they now retell the poem 'The Echoing Green' to their partners?
  ● Explain that this is a pictorial poem where life is symbolised by the beginning and end of a beautiful spring day. The poet signals the passage of time with the contrast made between youth and old age.

● Discuss the difficulties their partners found understanding the retelling. Did it have a recognisable beginning, middle or end? Agree as a class that the pictures and text and are in the wrong order. Ask the children to highlight the clues that show them the progression of the poem.
● Tell them to cut out the boxes and arrange them in the correct order with the beginning, middle and end labels stuck in the correct boxes.
● Next, ask for a volunteer in the class to retell the beginning of the poem in their own words, then someone else to retell the middle and another to retell the end of the poem.
● Now ask the class to retell the whole poem to their partners, using the rearranged boxes as a guide.

Comprehension

● **Photocopiable pages 24 and 25 'Blackbird'**
  ● This comprehension activity asks the children to think about the progression of beginning, middle and end within the extract as they answer and generate their own question.
  ● Hand out the photocopiable sheets to the children and ask them to read the poem. They may like to discuss it in groups before moving on to answer the questions.

What's on the CD-ROM

On the CD-ROM you will find:
● Printable versions of all three photocopiable pages.
● Answers to 'The Echoing Green' and 'Blackbird (2)'.
● Interactive version of 'The Echoing Green'.

Sequencing

The Echoing Green

■ Read the poem below. Does it make sense?

■ Cut out the boxes and arrange them in the correct order so that the poem makes sense. Use the labels provided at the foot of the page to help you.

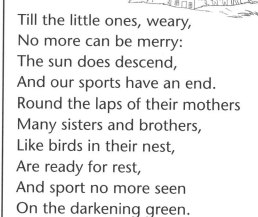

Old John, with white hair,
Does laugh away care,
Sitting under the oak,
Among the old folk.
They laugh at our play,
And soon they all say,
'Such, such were the joys
When we all, girls and boys,
In our youth-time were seen'
On the Echoing Green.

The sun does arise,
And make happy the skies;
The merry bell rings
To welcome the spring;
The skylark and thrush,
The birds of the bush,
Sing louder around
To the bell's cheerful sound;
While our sports shall be seen
On the Echoing Green.

Till the little ones, weary,
No more can be merry:
The sun does descend,
And our sports have an end.
Round the laps of their mothers
Many sisters and brothers,
Like birds in their nest,
Are ready for rest,
And sport no more seen
On the darkening green.

William Blake

Beginning	Middle
Middle	End

Sequencing

Blackbird (1)

My wife saw it first –
I was reading the evening paper.
Come and look, she said.

It was trying to drink
Where water had formed on a drain-cover.
It was shabby with dying.
It did not move until I was very close –
Then it hopped off, heavily,
Disturbing dead leaves.

We left water, crumbs.
It did not touch them
But waited among the leaves,
Silently.

This morning was beautiful:
Sunlight, other birds
Singing.

It was outside the door.
I picked it up
And it was like holding feathered air.
I wrapped what was left
Incongruously
In green sycamore leaves
And buried it near the tree,
Inches down.

This evening
I find it difficult to concentrate
On the paper, the news
Of another cosmonaut.

Christopher Leach

Text © Christopher Leach; illustrations © 2009, JHS Studio/Beehive Illustration.

PHOTOCOPIABLE   **SCHOLASTIC**
www.scholastic.co.uk

Sequencing

Blackbird (2)

1. Who disturbed the bird at the beginning of the poem? Why do you say that?

_____

_____

2. Did the poet and his wife try to make the bird comfortable overnight? How do you know that?

_____

_____

_____

3. What had happened to the bird by the morning?

_____

_____

4. What did the poet say he did before the end of the poem?

_____

_____

_____

5. How does the end of the story link to the beginning of the poem?

_____

_____

_____

6. Your question:

_____

_____

Your answer:

_____

Chapter 2

Literal questioning

Introduction

Literal questioning generally focuses on the characters, action and place that provide the basic elements of a story. It is the simplest and most direct of the three question types to generate and answer because it is found right there on the page. Literal information tells the reader *who* is in the picture or text, *what* they are doing, *where* it is happening (and sometimes *when* it is happening). The meaning is obvious to the reader and does not require interpretation.

Poster notes

PC Page always right there! (page 27)
The poster on page 27 serves as a useful classroom prompt throughout Chapter 2. It offers an analogy and guide that helps children to grasp the concept of 'being literal'. It shows them how to identify and apply literal thinking to gather 'who', 'what' and 'where' information and to answer and generate literal questions.

The children are introduced to PC Page from the Literacy Force whose job is to patrol the images and sentences in a book and write down everything she sees. She notes down what happens 'right there' in front of her.

In this chapter

	About the section	About the comprehension activity
Who? What? Where? page 28	Children answer literal questions that focus on characters, action and place in story narrative.	Children answer 'who', 'what' and 'where' questions about Lewis Carroll's *Alice in Wonderland*.
Literal questions page 32	Children focus on matching words and images to answer literal questions.	Children answer literal questions about *Peter and the Wolf* (story retold by Selina Hastings).
Answering literal questions page 36	Children answer 'who', 'what' and 'where' questions based on a text.	Children link information in *Falling Angels* by Colin Thompson to answer literal questions.
Skimming and scanning for literal meaning page 40	Children use skimming and scanning techniques to find key words in text and pictures.	Children match key words in *The Turbulent Term of Tyke Tiler* by Gene Kemp with the same words in literal questions.

Literal questioning

PC Page always right there!

Oh dear! I shall be late.

I note down the **who**, **what** and **where** that is right there!

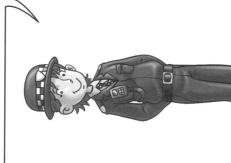

Suddenly a White Rabbit with pink eyes ran close by her on the bank.

PC Page: Who? What? Where? Right there!

PC Page knows where to look.
To write the facts down in her book.
She knows the literal **who**, **what** and **where**.
Are on the page – yes, right there!
She is always on the case.
Noting the character, action and place.

Illustrations © 2009, JHS Studio/Beehive Illustration.

Who? What? Where?

To identify literal information about characters within pictures and text. To gather, organise and classify this information to ask and answer questions.

Background knowledge

For children to successfully answer and generate literal questions they need to practise identifying and classifying the literal key words that are associated with characters, action and place on the page. To do this they need to ask themselves the questions that lead them to the key information in pictures and text. For example: *Who is this story about? What is happening to them? What are they doing? Where are they? Where is it happening?* This basic information helps the reader to gain the gist of a story or non-fiction passage and prepares them to respond to and generate their own questions.

Skills

Explain to the children that these activities will show them how to find information that will help them to ask and answer 'who', 'what' and 'where' questions.

● **Photocopiable page 29 'Alice in Wonderland'**
　● Explain that literal information is made up of words and images that are right there on the page. Literal meaning is obvious to the reader and it doesn't need interpretation.
　● Talk to the children about the purpose of locating and classifying 'who', 'what' and 'where' information. Explain that this is essential information that provides them with the main points of a story and gives them an idea of what the text is about before going into greater depth.

● Hand out the photocopiable sheet. Tell the children to read the passage with a partner. Ask them to imagine they are PC Page (see poster page 27) who has arrived at the scene of the story. Explain that they need to circle 'who' (noun) is in the story, 'what' (verb) the characters are doing and 'where' (noun) they are in different-coloured pens.
● Tell the children to gather these key words and write them into the correct boxes. This will provide them with basic sentences about the story from which they can practise asking questions for their partners to answer. For example: *Alice sat on the bank. Who sat on the bank?*

Comprehension

● **Photocopiable pages 30 and 31 'A mad tea party'**
　● Hand out the photocopiable sheets to the children. Ask them to read the extract from *Alice in Wonderland*.
　● Remind the children to highlight the 'who', 'what' and 'where' information as they read the passage to help them answer literal questions about the characters, action and setting of the story. They should then answer the questions.

 What's on the CD-ROM

On the CD-ROM you will find:
● Printable versions of all three photocopiable pages.
● Answers to 'Alice in Wonderland' and 'A mad tea party (2)'.
● Interactive version of 'Alice in Wonderland'.

Who? What? Where?

Alice in Wonderland

■ Highlight the **who**, **what** and **where** information in the text. Then put it in the correct columns in the chart.

■ Use the information to create questions for your partner.

Alice was beginning to get very tired of sitting by her sister on the bank, and of having nothing to do: once or twice she had peeped into the book her sister was reading, but it had no pictures or conversations in it, "and what is the use of a book," thought Alice, "without pictures or conversations?"

So she was considering in her own mind (as well as she could, for the hot day made her feel very sleepy and stupid) whether the pleasure of making a daisy-chain would be worth the trouble of getting up and picking the daisies, when suddenly a White Rabbit with pink eyes ran close by her.

Lewis Carroll

Who? (character) noun	What? (doing) verb	Where? (place) noun
Alice	was sitting next to her sister	on the bank

Illustrations © 2009, JHS Studio/Beehive Illustration.

Who? What? Where?

A mad tea party (1)

There was a table set out under a tree in front of the house, and the March Hare and the Hatter were having tea at it: a Dormouse was sitting between them, fast asleep, and the other two were resting their elbows on it, and talking over its head. "Very uncomfortable for the Dormouse," thought Alice; "only, as it's asleep, I suppose it doesn't mind."

The table was a large one, but the three were all crowded together at one corner of it. "No room! No room!" they all cried out when they saw Alice coming.

"There's *plenty* of room!" said Alice indignantly, and she sat down in a large armchair at one end of the table.

"Have some wine," the March Hare said in an encouraging tone.

Alice looked all round the table, but there was nothing on it but tea. "I don't see any wine," she remarked.

Lewis Carroll

Illustration © 1999, Helen Oxenbury.

Who? What? Where?

A mad tea party (2)

1. **What were the March Hare and Hatter doing under the tree?**

   _____

   _____

   _____

2. **Who was sitting between them, asleep?**

   _____

   _____

   _____

3. **Where was the table set out?**

   _____

   _____

   _____

4. **Who says that 'there is *plenty* of room'?**

   _____

   _____

   _____

5. **Your question:**

   _____

   _____

   Your answer:

   _____

   _____

   _____

Literal questions

Objectives

To identify and classify literal key word information about characters, action and place within text.
To respond to questions and formulate questions from text.

Background knowledge

This section introduces children to the process involved in asking their own basic literal questions. It is important to emphasise that if they can understand how these questions are generated, it will be much easier to answer them. Remind the children that literal questions usually begin with 'who', 'what' or 'where' and that the information and answers are there in the text and pictures.

Skills

This activity will show the children how to find matching key words in text quickly to help them find the answer to literal questions accurately and swiftly.

- **Photocopiable page 33 'The Russian composer'**
  - Tell the children that this activity builds on what they already know about gathering literal 'who', 'what' and 'where' information to ask questions.
  - To ask a literal question they simply need to replace the verb or noun in a statement with 'who', 'what' or 'where' and rearrange the words in the sentence. For example: *Who was Sergei Prokofiev? Sergei Prokofiev was a composer. Where did he return to? He returned to Russia. What did Prokofiev do for his son? Prokofiev adapted Peter and the Wolf for his son.*

- Hand out the photocopiable sheet and ask the children to read the text and look at the pictures that accompany it. Ask them to identify and underline the 'who', 'what' and 'where' key words in different-coloured pens. Following this, they may find it helpful to sort the information into headed columns (see photocopiable page 29 'Alice in Wonderland') before formulating their questions.
- Finally, ask them to generate their own questions and answers from the information they have gathered from the text.

Comprehension

- **Photocopiable pages 34 and 35 'Peter and the wolf'**
  - Hand out the photocopiable sheets. Suggest the children highlight the characters, action and place within the text as they read.
  - They should use this information to help them to ask and answer their own questions from the text.

What's on the CD-ROM

On the CD-ROM you will find:
- Printable versions of all three photocopiable pages.
- Answers to 'Peter and the wolf (2)'.
- Interactive version of 'Peter and the wolf'.

Literal questions

The Russian composer

The composer **Sergei Prokofiev** adapted the children's story *Peter and the Wolf* for his son in 1936 after his return to Russia. Each character in the story is represented by an instrument and musical theme and the story is told by a narrator who is accompanied by an **orchestra**.

Characters and instruments

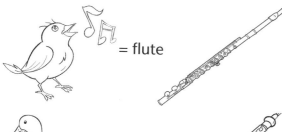 = flute

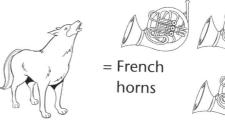 = French horns

 = oboe

 = timpani and bass drum

 = clarinet

= bassoon

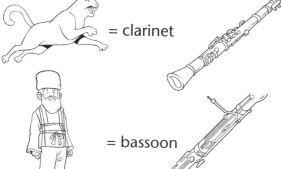

 = string instruments

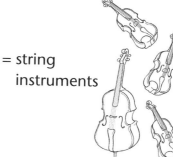

■ Underline the **who**, **what** and **where** information above to create your own literal questions on a separate sheet of paper.

For example:
Question: Who adapted the children's story *Peter and the Wolf*?
Answer: *Sergei Prokofiev* adapted the children's story *Peter and the Wolf*.

Illustrations © 2009, JHS Studio/Beehive Illustration.

Name:

Peter and the wolf (1)

Peter lived with his grandfather in a little house in the middle of one of the great Russian forests. The forest was a dark place and during the winter, when the snow lay thickly on the ground, it could be dangerous. On still nights the howling of the wolves rose clearly into the icy air. But Peter's home was in a pleasant clearing. It was surrounded by a garden around which ran a high stone wall. On the other side of the wall were a meadow and a pond. Every morning Peter would come whistling down the path and through the gate, which he carelessly left open, his pockets full of bread to feed the duck who lived on the pond.

Text © 1987, Selina Hastings; illustration © 1987, Reg Cartwright.

Literal questions

Peter and the wolf (2)

1. Who lived in the middle of a Russian forest?

    _____

    _____

2. Where was Peter's home?

    _____

    _____

3. What happened on still nights?

    _____

    _____

4. What was Peter doing when he left open the gate?

    _____

    _____

5. Write a question to match the answer.

    _____

    _____

    Answer: Peter's home was surrounded by a garden.

6. Write a question to match the answer.

    _____

    Answer: Peter kept the bread for the duck in his pockets.

7. Your question:

    _____

    _____

    Your answer:

    _____

    _____

Answering literal questions

Objective

To identify literal key words in the question and locate the same word(s) in the text and link them to the picture to find the answer.

Background knowledge

This section explains the process involved in answering more complex literal questions. Some questions ask the reader to gather literal information from different parts of the text and link them to picture information to give full answers.

Once children understand the technique involved, they will find literal questions quite straightforward to answer. They just need to remember that the same sentence or key words that are used in the question are also there in the text and may be linked to the picture. When they are able to locate these words and link them to the text or images, they will find the answer to the 'who', 'what' and 'where' questions are always nearby.

Skills

Explain to the children that these activities will show them how to gather 'who', 'what' and 'where' information correctly to answer literal questions from text and pictures.
- **Photocopiable page 37 'Laughing Cavalier'**
  - Explain to the children that they are going to answer more complex 'who', 'what' and 'where' literal questions.

- Remind them that to answer a simple 'who' question they replace the 'who' word at the front of the question with the character's identity: *Who is happy? Billy is happy.* To answer a 'where' question: begin with the subject of the enquiry and end with the answer: *Where is Helen? Helen is at home.* To answer a 'what' question: rearrange the order of the words to make a statement: *What is Jade doing in the pool? Jade is swimming in the pool.*
- To answer more complex questions, the children need to look directly in the text for the same words that form part of the question. Sometimes these words are spread around different parts of the text. Answers may also be linked to pictures.
- Hand out the photocopiable sheet. Ask the children to read the text and picture information.
- Tell them to read each question, search the text for the same words that are in italics in the questions, underline these words, re-read the question and return to the underlined text. They will find the answer to the question close by.

Comprehension

- **Photocopiable pages 38 and 39 'Falling angels'**
  - Give the children the photocopiable sheets. Ask them to read the text in pairs.
  - Tell them to look for the answers using words from the question that are there in the text to guide them to the answer.

What's on the CD-ROM

On the CD-ROM you will find:
- Printable versions of all three photocopiable pages.
- Answers to 'Laughing Cavalier' and 'Falling angels (2)'.
- Interactive versions of 'Laughing Cavalier' and 'Falling angels'.

Laughing Cavalier

The artist who created the cheeky version (on the left) of one of the most famous portraits in the world has **added** something **to the original composition**. The picture is based on the **Laughing Cavalier** (1624) which is a famous oil painting by the Dutch artist Frans Hals. The title of the Hals painting dates from the Victorian era when it was first named by Sir Richard Wallace and shown to the public in London.

Example:

Question: What has been added to the original composition?

Answer: A cat has been added to the original composition.

1. **What** is this *picture based on*?
2. **Who** is the *famous artist*?
3. **Who** *first named* the painting?
4. **When** was the painting *first shown to the public*?
5. **Where** was Hals' painting *first shown*?

Left-hand image © Donna Thomson; right-hand image © The Bridgeman Art Library.

Name:

Falling angels (1)

The first time Sally saw someone else flying, she was seven. Her mother was sleeping in the warm summer afternoon. Beside her in the grass her baby brother Peter curled up in her shadow. As Sally floated over the garden, she saw the baby stretch out and rise into the air.

Maybe it's just us, she thought, something special about our family.

Text and illustration © 2001, Colin Thompson.

Answering literal questions

Falling angels (2)

1. Who saw someone else flying when she was seven?

   _____

2. Who was curled up in his mother's shadow?

   _____

3. Where was Sally's mother lying?

   _____

4. Where was Sally when she saw the baby rise into the air?

   _____

5. What was Sally's mother doing in the warm afternoon?

   _____

6. Your question:

   _____

   _____

   Your answer:

   _____

   _____

7. Your question:

   _____

   _____

   Your answer:

   _____

   _____

Skimming and scanning for literal meaning

To answer literal questions from text by skimming and scanning to locate the same words as the key words that appear in the question.

Background knowledge

When the children are confident with gathering key literal information, it is helpful for them to become practised at skimming and scanning. Skimming is used for identifying the main ideas of a text, and scanning involves searching for key words and ideas within a long passage and illustration that link to key words in a question. These skills help children to answer literal questions with accuracy, confidence and speed, and also prepare them to generate their own questions successfully.

Skimming and scanning skills also help children to acquaint themselves quickly with the basic plot of a story or a play. However, it is important to remind the children that these skills are only used for gathering information quickly – they are no substitute for real reading. Eyes passing over the words is not reading; reading involves engaging actively with the meaning of each word in context, asking questions and noting detail.

Skills

Explain to the children that these activities will show them how to find information that will help them to answer 'who', 'what' and 'where' literal questions swiftly and accurately.

- **Photocopiable page 41 'A mad tea party play'**
  - Tell the children that to acquaint themselves with the basic plot of a story and answer literal questions from text easily, accurately and speedily, they need to practise skimming and scanning skills.

- Explain that these skills will help them to gather information and match the key words in the questions with the same words in the text to help them answer questions.
- Hand out the photocopiable sheet. Read and discuss the play together.
- From the list of words provided below the playscript, ask the children to quickly locate and underline each word in the text as they find them. Explain that they need to skim left to right and scan up and down to find the words. Encourage them to say the word they are looking for in their heads, look for the initial letter and remember the shape and length of the word.
- In pairs, ask the children to skim and scan the text to answer the literal questions on the bottom of the page, using the words they have underlined and the question words in bold to guide their answer.

Comprehension

- **Photocopiable pages 42 and 43 'The turbulent term of Tyke Tiler'**
  - Hand out the photocopiable sheets. Tell the children to read the play in small groups, each taking a different part: narrator, Mr Merchant, Harlequin and Tyke.
  - Once they have done this, ask the children to skim and scan the play for the key question words in italics. These words are there in the text and will guide them to the answer.

What's on the CD-ROM

On the CD-ROM you will find:
- Printable versions of all three photocopiable pages.
- Answers to 'A mad tea party play' and 'The turbulent term of Tyke Tyler (2)'.
- Interactive version of 'A mad tea party play'.

Skimming and scanning for literal meaning

A mad tea party play

Scene One

Lights go up to reveal a large table laid out for afternoon tea. There are seats set for ten people. At one end of the table is an armchair. Only two seats are occupied, one by the Mad Hatter and the other by the March Hare. Sitting between them, fast asleep, is the Dormouse.

The March Hare and the Mad Hatter drink their tea. The Hatter puts down his teacup and leans towards the Hare and mutters something. He rests his elbow on the Dormouse as he does so. The Hare replies and he too leans on the Dormouse.

Alice *(quietly to herself)*: Very uncomfortable for the Dormouse. Only, as it's asleep, I suppose it doesn't mind.

March Hare and **Mad Hatter** *(together loudly)*: No room! No room!

Alice *(indignantly)*: There's *plenty* of room!

Alice sits down in the armchair, crosses her legs and looks at the others.

■ Skim and scan the text to find the following key words in the playscript. Underline each word in the text as you find it.

armchair	March Hare	teacup	No room!	Dormouse	Alice

■ Skim and scan for the words in bold. Use these and the underlined words to answer the following questions on another sheet of paper.

1. What is at **one end of the table**?

2. Who occupies the **other** seat?

3. What does the Hatter **put down** before he **mutters something**?

4. Where does he **rest his elbow**?

5. What do the March Hare and Mad Hatter say **together loudly**?

6. Who is **indignant**?

Name:

The turbulent term of Tyke Tiler (1)

Act 1

Scene 1

Enter in front of curtains **Mr Merchant (Sir)** *who sees audience and addresses them.*

Sir   Hello. Afternoon play is over. It's a good time for a story. This is a tale of a turbulent term. Tyke Tiler's term. Tyke told it to me when all the upset had died down, and now we tell it to you.

Loud school buzzer rings.

Our play is about to begin so…

Sir nearly gets bowled over by a Harlequin clown turning cartwheels.

Harlequin   Sorry, Sir! But we got to have the jokes in. Tyke's idea.

Sir   *(holding head in hands)*: Go on then.

Harlequin   *(to audience)*: What did the cross-eyed teacher say? I can't control my pupils.

(Groans – taped.)

Harlequin cartwheels away. Sir walks to desks as class file in, noisily.

Lights dim as all sit down. Spotlight turns to **Tyke** *and* **Danny** *still outside door.* **Tyke** *and* **Danny** *are wearing jeans, T-shirt and trainers.* **Tyke** *is carrying a tea-money tin. Tyke is an alert independent twelve-year-old. Danny lives under Tyke's protection. He is not bright and develops a bad stutter when nervous and then only Tyke knows what he is saying.* **Danny** *grabs Tyke's arm and shows Tyke a ten pound note.*

Tyke   Where didja get that, you nutter?

The turbulent term of Tyke Tiler (2)

1. Who is Mr Merchant addressing?

   _____

   _____

2. What rings?

   _____

   _____

3. What is it 'a good time for'?

   _____

   _____

4. Who says it was Tyke's idea?

   _____

   _____

5. What is taped?

   _____

   _____

6. As the spotlight turns to Tyke and Danny, where are they?

   _____

   _____

7. Who has a ten pound note?

   _____

   _____

Chapter 3

Prediction

Introduction

Prediction is an essential skill that combines literal and inferential thinking and helps children to monitor their comprehension. It also informs teachers of the children's ability to use background knowledge, text clues, picture clues and knowledge of story structure to make meaning from text.

Use of prediction encourages children to think more flexibly before, during and after reading. However, to gain the most from prediction, they must be taught explicitly how and when to predict and why they need these skills.

Poster notes

Forensic Fred the police predictor (page 45)
Prediction encourages children to make links between clues, prior knowledge and guesswork to make meaning from text as they read. It helps them to deduce possible outcomes from vital small clues on the page that are like fingerprints left at the scene of a crime. They point to who is involved, what they have been doing, where they have been, what may happen next and why, from the evidence found.

Forensic Fred is a useful analogy to help children grasp the tricky concept of foretelling from evidence and justifying reasons given from the clues they have gathered that link to prior knowledge.

In this chapter

	About the section	About the comprehension
Cause and effect page 46	Children gather cause-and-effect clues that suggest the reasons why things happen or might happen.	Children answer questions about *Pirate Diary* by Richard Platt and then predict the outcome.
Anticipating before and after page 50	Children look at how logical predictions help to monitor their comprehension.	Children make predictions from clues and answer questions about FE Higgins' *Black Book of Secrets*.
Clues from the cover page 54	Children make predictions from information on the book cover about the contents of the book.	Children use information on the cover of *Tales of Mystery and Madness* by Edgar Allan Poe to answer questions.
Predicting meaning from symbolic images page 58	Children make meaning from images to support comprehension.	Children predict the meaning and purpose of a variety of road sign symbols.

Prediction

Forensic Fred the police predictor

Forensic Fred can see where a story might have begun or where it might end.

I can see the 'whole picture' from little clues. I ask:
Who and what is this about?
What are they doing?
Where are they?
I ask **why** questions to predict what will happen next from what I know – to work out what I don't know... I can say **how** I know from the clues I find.

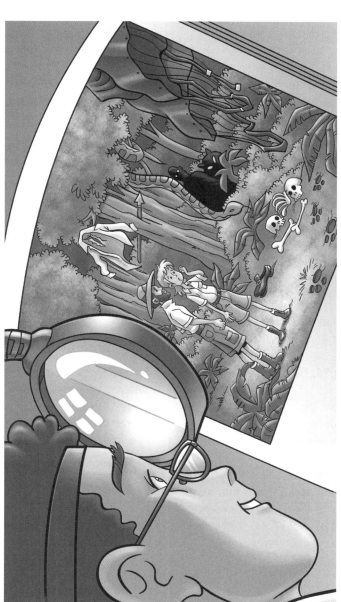

"They said they'd meet us here. I wonder what has happened to them."

Sometimes Forensic Fred has a picture of the whole story long before the full story has been told, and from the evidence that the clues provide he can forecast what might have happened before and what might happen next...

Cause and effect

To find clues from images and words that suggest what might happen next.

To predict story outcomes that they can justify with confidence, children need to understand the meaning of cause and effect. They need to know that the 'effect' is what happens, the 'cause' is the reason why it happens and the conjunction 'because' links the two together. When they understand this, they will be able to explain how actions produce consequences and how a series of incidents can be created from one action. These invaluable investigative skills help them to calculate what may happen next from what has happened before, and why. It relies on a process of literal and inferential thinking, questioning and reasoning that links to their prior knowledge, personal experience, and clues offered by the author and illustrator.

Explain to the children that these activities will show them how to predict the flow of events in a story narrative.

● **Photocopiable page 47 'This happened because of that'**

● Talk to the children about the purpose of prediction and how some actions have outcomes that can be anticipated. For example, if you leave toast under the grill too long, it will burn.

● Discuss everyday cause and effect situations. Encourage the children to talk about things that have happened to them because of their actions or the actions of others.

● Hand out the photocopiable sheet. Explain the term 'cause and effect'. Tell the children that *what* happens is called 'effect' and *why* it happens is the 'cause'. When both are linked together by the word 'because', a reason is given for the prediction. For example, *I had extra chores to do because I didn't tidy up when Mum asked me to.*

● Ask the children to read the jumbled pair of phrases given. They are split into two parts on the page under the headings 'effect' and 'cause'. Tell them to re-organise these statements into sensible sentences that explain why something has happened using the conjunction 'because'.

● Then tell them to practise this further by completing the activities that follow on the page.

● Finally, ask the children to predict the final outcome for each 'effect and cause' sentence they have written.

● **Photocopiable pages 48 and 49 'Pirate diary'**

● Hand out the photocopiable sheets. Encourage the children to talk about the clues in the picture and text that they can see, in small groups or pairs.

● Then ask them to answer the prediction questions and generate their own questions and answers.

On the CD-ROM you will find:
● Printable versions of all three photocopiable pages.
● Answers to 'This happened because of that' and 'Pirate diary (2)'.
● Interactive version of 'This happened because of that'.

Cause and effect

This happened because of that

■ Match the cause with the effect.

This happened…   *because*… of that.

Effect   **Cause**

1. The football crowd booed.   Jenny couldn't eat another thing.
2. I had extra chores to do.   Dad had left the fish uncovered.
3. The cat ate our supper.   The star player was sent off the pitch.
4. Sam finished Jenny's plateful.   I didn't tidy up when Mum asked me to.

1. _____

2. _____

3. _____

4. _____

■ Write your own cause to complete the following sentences.

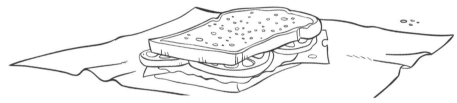

Effect: My sandwich was gritty with sand because

Cause: _____

Effect: _____

Cause: A snowstorm was on its way.

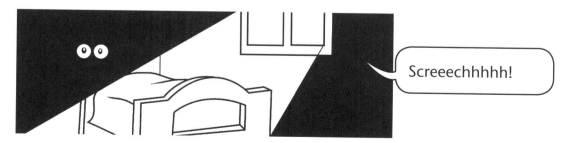

Screeechhhhh!

James felt frightened because he heard a shrill noise in the dark.

Effect: _____

Cause: _____

Illustrations © 2009, JHS Studio/Beehive Illustration.

Name:

Pirate diary (1)

"Damn your eyes, you treacherous rogues, STOP THEM!" Our captain's voice cut through the smoke and the pirates' yells. "Make sail! Make sail! Steer hard to port!" As the smoke drifted away I could see that the crewmen close by seemed not to hear his words. To my puzzlement they merely stepped back as the pirates boarded.

The first to leap across was a tall, red-bearded man dressed in a fine frock-coat. He led a crowd of perhaps twenty pirates towards the quarterdeck. There had been some half-dozen people on it before the attack began. Now all were gone except our captain and second mate. The pair of them had drawn their swords and pistols.

Cause and effect

Pirate diary (2)

1. Explain why you think the crewmen stepped back as the pirates boarded.

   _____

   _____

2. Why do you think the captain shouted "Make sail! Make sail! Steer hard to port!"?

   _____

   _____

3. Predict what you think will happen next to the remaining crew members and say why.

   _____

   _____

4. Your prediction question:

   _____

   _____

   Your answer:

   _____

   _____

5. Your prediction question:

   _____

   _____

   Your answer:

   _____

   _____

Anticipating before and after

Objective

To look for clues in text that suggest what may have happened before and what might happen next.

Background knowledge

When children are encouraged to make predictions before, during and after reading, it provides them with the perfect opportunity to monitor their comprehension. However, it is important that teachers draw their attention to specific contextual features for making predictions, rather than simply asking them to guess an outcome. Context clues in the text help the reader to make links with the author's intention based on prior experience and knowledge of people and consequences. These clues have meanings that are usually associated with each other or the general theme within a passage. They describe characters' feelings, intentions and actions which suggest to the reader what has gone before and help them to think ahead logically as they read to calculate what will happen next in a story. This process absorbs readers in what is possible and asks them to make reasoned justifications for their thinking.

Skills

Explain to the children that these activities will show them how to predict what has happened before and what might happen next from the picture and word clues.

- **Photocopiable page 51 'Before, now, next '**
  - Explain to the children that when they make predictions about outcomes, they are not only asked to think ahead using their own experience and knowledge, but also required to guess what may have happened before from clues in the text.
  - Hand out the photocopiable sheet. Ask the children to talk about the theme of the story (memory) and the clues in the text that link to the information in bold about Josie's situation.

Ask: *What do you know about her character that helps you to predict what she will do next? What does she find difficult to do? How does she solve a problem?*
- Tell the children to write the clues in the box that refer to what she has done 'before', then what she may do 'next' from the clues given in the 'story situation'.
- Ask them to write what they think will happen in the end, giving detailed reasons for the conclusion of the story.
- Working with partners or in groups, tell the children to follow this example and write their own short story situation, including prediction clues for other groups to gather to help them anticipate what will happen next and in the end.

Comprehension

- **Photocopiable pages 52 and 53 'Black book of secrets'**
  - Hand out the first photocopiable sheet. Ask the children to circle the clues in the text that suggest what may happen next.
  - Then hand out the second photocopiable sheet. Tell the children to answer the questions and to generate their own questions and answers.

 What's on the CD-ROM

On the CD-ROM you will find:
- Printable versions of all three photocopiable pages.
- Answers to 'Black book of secrets (2)'.
- Interactive version of 'Before, now, next'.

Before, now, next

■ Read the text below and the story situation. Complete the before box using the text as a guide. From this information can you predict what might happen next? Write your ideas in the next box.

■ In stories like this one, what usually happens in the end? Answer the questions at the bottom of the sheet.

Theme: Memory

No, that's not right – how did it go again?

Josie loves telling jokes but she never remembers the punchline. She just makes it up. She says she is **confident** about her first **big part** in the school play, but I can't help wondering what will happen when she has so **many lines**.

Clues box

Before	Story situation	Next
	Confident about her first part in a play that has lots of lines.	

What do you think happens in the end?

_____

_____

_____

Why do you say that?

_____

_____

_____

Illustrations © 2009, JHS Studio/Beehive Illustration.

Name:

Black book of secrets (1)

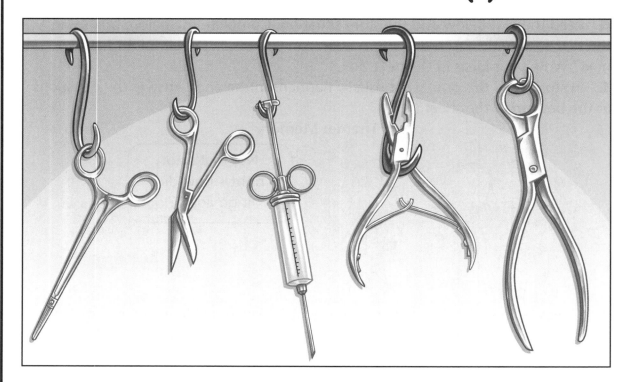

Fragment from the Memoirs of Ludlow Fitch

When I opened my eyes I knew that nothing in my miserable life prior to that moment could possibly be as bad as what was about to happen. I was lying on the cold earthen floor of a basement room lit by a single candle, no more than an hour's burning left. Instruments of a medical nature hung from hooks on the beams. Dark stains on the floor suggested blood. But it was the chair against the opposite wall that confirmed by suspicions. Thick leather straps attached to the arms and the legs were there for one purpose only: to hold down an unwilling patient. Ma and Pa were standing over me.

"'E's awake," crowed Ma excitedly.

Pa dragged me to my feet. He had me in an iron grip, my arm wrenched up behind my back. Ma held me by the hair. I looked from one to the other. Their grinning faces were only inches away from mine. I knew I should not look to them to save me.

Another man, concealed until now in the shadows, stepped forward and took me by the chin. He forced open my mouth and ran a blackened foul-tasting finger around my gums.

"How much?" asked Pa, drooling with anticipation.

"Not bad," said the man. "Thrupence apiece. Maybe twelve in all."

"It's a deal," said Pa. "Who needs teeth anyway?"

"Someone, I hope," replied the man drily. "I sell 'em for a living."

Text © 2007, F.E. Higgins; illustrations © 2009, JHS Studio/Beehive Illustration.

Black book of secrets (2)

1. What sort of people were Ma and Pa? Why do you say that?

_____

_____

2. How long do you predict the boy had been lying in the basement room? Explain why you say that.

_____

_____

_____

3. Do you think the boy was surprised by his parents' actions? What are the clues that suggest this to you?

_____

_____

4. Your prediction question:

_____

_____

Your answer:

_____

_____

5. Your prediction question:

_____

_____

Your answer:

_____

_____

Clues from the cover

To be able to link visual clues, key words in the title and genre to make predictions.

Background knowledge

This section shows how discussion about clues from a book cover is a particularly effective way to elicit predictions from children. Once they have an idea of the different types and categories of writing known as 'genre' and can differentiate between them, they are able to figure out genre and theme from the title and pictures on the cover. They also know whether the contents are fiction or non-fiction, and whether it is a subject they like and already know about. In addition, cover information usually suggests the sort of vocabulary they may need to know. The book title and subheadings generally provide key word clues about the contents and theme of the book, whereas the cover picture tends to offer more inferred information about the characters and events inside.

Skills

Explain to the children that these activities will show them how to anticipate genre and story narrative from clues given in titles and pictures.

- **Photocopiable page 55 'Book covers'**
  - Show the children a range of fiction books and explain the meaning of 'genre'.
  - Tell them that they are going to search for genre clues and other details on the cover to help them predict the contents of the story.
  - Unlike non-fiction material (designed explicitly to inform the reader), story books rely on title and illustrations to infer and indicate the story theme and contents.

- Hand out the photocopiable sheet. Read and discuss the list of different genre features with the class. Ask them to talk in groups about their favourite books and genre. What are the main features of these book covers?
- Ask the children to look at the table of titles and then write the genre they think is represented by each title in the labelled boxes, giving their reasons under the heading 'Justification'.
- Ask pairs to choose a title (or make up their own) and, using the title information, discuss and illustrate a cover that suggests the contents of the book on a separate sheet of paper.
- Tell the children to label and justify the clues and features of their cover that suggest what the story contents are about, such as imagery, title, font style and illustration.

Comprehension

- **Photocopiable pages 56 and 57 'Tales of mystery and madness'**
  - Hand out the first photocopiable sheet. Ask the children to look at the cover and read the annotations. Ask them to add to and justify the annotations.
  - Now hand out the second photocopiable sheet. Ask the children to answer the questions and generate questions that reflect their predictions about the book's contents from the cover.

What's on the CD-ROM

On the CD-ROM you will find:
- Printable versions of all three photocopiable pages.
- Answers to 'Tales of mystery and madness (2)'.
- Interactive versions of 'Book covers' and 'Tales of mystery and madness'.

Clues from the cover

Book covers

■ The following are examples of different kinds of text and their characteristics.

Humorous: Aimed to make the audience laugh, the plots usually include funny mishaps, surprises and sub-plots set against a backdrop of everyday life.

Science fiction: Involves ideas beyond present-day scientific reality. Technical language and invented words such as 'starship' and 'intergalactic'.

Myth/legend: About values and beliefs of ancient civilisations and different cultures. Inspirational stories of heroics passed down through generations.

Fantasy: Set in 'other worlds' full of mythical creatures, witches and warlocks and so on, where magic and the supernatural are considered normal.

Historical/classic: Involves fictional characters in a plot that revolves around historical events or a period of history.

Mystery: About characters who try to discover vital information to solve a problem. Clues and detective work uncover hidden truths at the climax of the story and end in resolution.

Horror: Dark fictional tales intended to unsettle, horrify and shock the audience. Descriptions of gruesome or supernatural events where goblins, monsters, ghosts and so on intrude into human everyday life.

Fairy story: Far-fetched events – hero and heroine; good and evil. Traditional story characters: princes/princesses, witches, dragons.

Adventure: Twisting, turning plot, constant excitement and danger, a series of complicated/difficult events and problems, full of suspense.

■ Look at the book titles below. Write which genre matches the titles and give your reasons why.

Fiction book titles	Genre	Justification (reasons why)
Forever and a Day		
House of Shadows		
Pickles Sniffs It Out		
A Broomstick Too Far		
Big Biscuit		
The Goblin Ultimatum		
Storm Bringer		
The Frog Princess		
Alien Mist		
The War Horse		
Burpy Murphy and Other Nonsense Tales		

Clues from the cover

Tales of mystery and madness (1)

Clue-words in title

Style of font

Expression and colour of moon

Clues from author's name

Clues from illustrator's name

Clues from images

Clues from images

Clues from expression and colour of man's features

Illustration © 2003, Gris Grimly.

Clues from the cover

Tales of mystery and madness (2)

1. What genre do you think this book is? Why do you say that?

    _____

    _____

2. How many stories are in this book – one or more than one? How do you know that?

    _____

    _____

3. Your question:

    _____

    _____

    Your answer:

    _____

    _____

4. Your question:

    _____

    _____

    Your answer:

    _____

    _____

5. Your question:

    _____

    _____

    Your answer:

    _____

    _____

Predicting meaning from symbolic images

Objective

Making sense of symbolic picture clues to predict purpose, meaning and possible outcomes.

Background knowledge

Asking children to clarify purpose, meanings and ideas from the inferred clues within generic picture information found in everyday signs and symbols is a helpful way to hone their prediction skills. Signs and symbols give us instant warning, information and instruction, using few words. Their simple bold picture silhouettes and symbolic shapes are usually a logical replacement for the written word – and are generally easy to interpret. The warnings they offer draw attention to potential danger and ask the reader to predict what might happen if the sign is ignored.

It is interesting to note that these simple images are used internationally to inform people of all ages and languages. They not only signal danger but also help people to identify facilities, such as restaurants (knife and fork), telephones (silhouette of handset), or rest rooms (silhouette of a man or woman).

Skills

These activities will show children how to predict purpose, meaning and possible outcomes from combined key word clues and images.

- **Photocopiable page 59 'What does it mean?'**
  - Explain that symbols and signs are around the home and in the outside world to warn, inform and guide.
  - Talk about how images can suggest something without words. Explain that symbols for feelings, actions, events, places and so on are often represented by simple drawings of objects that are linked to these things in some way.
  - Hand out the photocopiable sheet. Ask the children to talk in pairs about the meaning, purpose and impact of each picture symbol.

- Ask them to cut out the cards and to write the meaning for each symbol on them. Then to sort the cards into three categories to show and whether it instructs, informs or warns.
- Talk about categories of these symbols. For example: a crumbling cliff *warning* of falling rocks; a bicycle with a red line through it *instructing* you 'not to cycle here'; a knife and fork *informing* you of somewhere to eat.
- In pairs, invite the children to predict what might happen if some of the warning signs were ignored.
- Finally, on another sheet of paper, ask groups of children to create and design a playground or a park, with appropriate signs and symbols.

Comprehension

- **Photocopiable pages 60 and 61 'Road signs'**
  - Hand out the first photocopiable sheet. The children need to look for clues represented by the images to predict meanings. Ask the children to first identify the signs and then think of their purpose.
  - Then hand out the second photocopiable sheet and ask the children to answer the questions and to generate and answer their own question.

What's on the CD-ROM

On the CD-ROM you will find:
- Printable versions of all three photocopiable pages.
- Answers to all three photocopiable pages.
- Interactive versions of 'What does it mean?' and 'Road signs'.

Predicting meaning from symbolic images

What does it mean?

■ Cut out these cards and stick them on another sheet of paper. Below each card write what they mean and whether their purpose is to instruct, inform or warn.

Illustrations © 2009, JHS Studio/Beehive Illustration.

Name:

Road signs (1)

Illustrations © 2009, JHS Studio/Beehive Illustration.

Predicting meaning from symbolic images

Road signs (2)

1. Explain why we have road signs.

   _____

   _____

2. Choose a sign that you think warns of danger. Explain why you have chosen that sign and what might happen if the motorist ignored the warning.

   _____

   _____

3. Explain what you think the symbol of a deer means on a sign and where you are likely to see this sign.

   _____

   _____

4. There is danger from flooding on a road near your house. Design a sign to show this.

   +---+
   | |
   | |
   | |
   | |
   | |
   | |
   +---+

5. Explain why you think this design would be an effective warning.

   _____

   _____

6. Your prediction question:

   _____

   _____

   Your answer:

   _____

Chapter 4

Inference

Introduction

This chapter focuses on the skills necessary to become an effective text detective. Children are shown how to identify the inference clues that highlight the author's hidden and implied meaning within text and pictures. They are shown how the inference process involves prediction skills and detective work to help them delve deeper than a literal 'who', 'what' and 'where' enquiry. The sections explain how to search for contextual clues and evidence within text or pictures to form conclusions and justify answers. They see how the process entails their own prior knowledge, personal experience, and knowledge of explicitly stated information and implied information to ask and answer their own inference questions accurately and confidently.

Poster notes

Being a text detective (page 63)
Once they are able to identify key information and predict cause and effect, the children can be shown how to answer and ask inference questions. This poster is a useful classroom display to use throughout this chapter, as the detective analogy helps to remind the children of the thinking involved in inferential enquiry.

The Text Detective can go further in text and picture investigation than PC Page, the literal officer. The Text Detective thinks and searches for key clues that are hidden and finds the evidence from the pictures and text to prove his case.

In this chapter

	About the section	About the comprehension
Inferred non-fiction clues page 64	Children identify images and words that are inferred.	Children identify literal or inferred questions about the evacuation in *Ethel and Ernest* by Raymond Briggs.
Seeking evidence from pictures and text page 68	Children gather inferred information and evidence from picture narrative and text.	Children answer questions about a poem entitled 'Pearls' by Jean Little.
Presenting evidence page 72	Children present evidence to justify answers given to inference questions.	Children give reasoned answers to questions about a bird box leaflet and generate their own questions.
Inference questions page 76	Children ask and answer inference questions based on a text.	Children use *Ways to Live Forever* by Sally Nichols to generate questions with justified answers.

Inference

Being a text detective

hoof marks near flower bed
+ part of glove near flower bed
+ trail of petals leading to hole in hedge
+ goat chewing glove
= **goat eating pink flowers.**

?

The Text Detective

I arrive on the story scene
After PC Page has been.
I search in text and pictures too
To ask **how** and **why** about each clue.
I skim and scan as I go
Gathering evidence to show 'how I know'.

Illustrations © 2009, JHS Studio/Beehive Illustration.

Inferred non-fiction clues

Objective

To identify and interpret inferred meaning from picture and text clues to better understand the author's meaning, and answer inference questions.

Background knowledge

An autobiography or biography is a form of non-fiction writing that also involves storytelling based on real events and facts about the life of the writer or another person. Many biographies are survival stories which children are drawn to because they describe the lives of people who have managed to overcome difficult childhoods to become successful adults. They find them inspirational and reassuring as they approach an age where responsibility increases and their actions have repercussions. Photographs are often used to illustrate the people and events in these stories. However, on rare occasions biographies are presented in graphic form – where pictures and speech bubbles replace the normal format, such as the comprehension activity this chapter focuses on.

This section explains how to find inferred word and picture clues from non-fiction information and shows the children how to distinguish between being literal and being inferential. Emphasis is also placed on the importance of gathering evidence from clues in the information to explain deductions.

Skills

Explain to the children that these activities will show them how to find clues that will help them to give reasoned answers to inference questions about non-fiction information.

● **Photocopiable page 65 'Every picture tells a story'**

● Discuss with the class how autobiographies and biographies are a form of non-fiction writing that combines literal facts with inferred information to produce an interesting account of someone's life story.

● Ask the children to consider the difference between being literal and using inference.

● Explain that when they can no longer ask 'who', 'what' and 'where' questions about what they can see on the page, they need to look deeper for inferred clues that only hint at meaning. They will then have to make connections with other information in the picture or the text, using their own knowledge to help them find meaning.

● Remind them that they always need to prove or explain how they know something.

● Hand out the photocopiable sheet. Ask the children to look at the picture and text to find literal information that they can generate questions about.

● Then ask them to search for inferred clues that explain what is happening and to circle them. Encourage them to discuss their findings in pairs.

● Finally, ask the children to complete the questions at the bottom of the sheet. Remind them that they need to explain how they know from the clues in the picture and the characters' dialogue.

Comprehension

● **Photocopiable pages 66 and 67 'Ethel and Ernest'**

● Hand out the photocopiable sheets. Ask the children to read the text and explain to them that this is a true story and is non-fiction text presented as a graphic novel.

● Ask the children to think about the difference between gathering literal information and inferred clues to answer the literal and inference questions correctly from the text and picture.

What's on the CD-ROM

On the CD-ROM you will find:
● Printable versions of all three photocopiable pages.
● Answers to 'Every picture tells a story' and 'Ethel and Ernest (2)'.
● Interactive version of 'Ethel and Ernest'.

Every picture tells a story

We should have moved to the country last year.

I heard them come over. It sounded like there were hundreds of them.

We had everyone in the shelter last night. Thank goodness!

■ What literal questions would PC Page ask?

Who?_____

What?_____

Where?_____

■ Find and circle the inference clues in the picture and in the text that explains what is happening. Then answer the questions below.

1. Why is the house so badly damaged? How do you know that?

_____

_____

2. Is this story set in modern times? Explain how you know.

_____

_____

Illustrations © 2009, JHS Studio/Beehive Illustration.

Name:

Ethel and Ernest (1)

Text and illustrations © 1998, Raymond Briggs.

PHOTOCOPIABLE

SCHOLASTIC
www.scholastic.co.uk

Inferred non-fiction clues

Ethel and Ernest (2)

- ■ Tick the PC Page box if it is a literal question.
- ■ Tick the Text Detective box if it is an inference question.
- ■ Then answer the question in full.

1. How many children are to be evacuated?

_____

_____

_____

2. Who is giving a speech to the nation on the radio? Explain how you know that.

_____

_____

_____

3. Who said "They're not taking ours away!"?

_____

_____

_____

4. Why was the boy being sent away? How do you know that?

_____

_____

_____

5. What clues tell you that life is very different for him away from home? Explain why you say that.

_____

_____

_____

_____

Illustrations © 2009, JHS Studio/Beehive Illustration.

Seeking evidence from pictures and text

Objective

To identify inferred meaning from text clues and images to use as evidence to support deduction.

Background knowledge

This section builds on the inference skills that the children have learned in the previous section. It explains how to find inferred word and picture clues from information and shows the children how to gather evidence from hidden and implied clues to support their deductions.

It may be helpful to refer the children again to poster page 63 'Being a text detective' to remind them that they can delve deeper to find answers to inference questions than PC Page, the literal officer, who can only see what is right there.

Skills

Explain to the children that these activities will show them how to find clues that enable them to give reasoned answers to inference questions about images and text.

● **Photocopiable page 69 'Making meaning from clues'**

● Explain that authors and illustrators often use clues that hint at meaning within text and pictures to make their writing more interesting.

● The clues they introduce ask the reader to think about and search for connections between their own knowledge and the key words and images given to infer meaning and make deductions.

● Explain that when a detective infers from these clues and makes deductions he must also be able to provide evidence to prove how he knows something.

● Hand out the photocopiable sheet to the children. Ask them to look at the picture, read the text and search for key information that will explain who is involved, what is happening and where the characters may have just returned from in this story.

● Ask the children to highlight or circle any clues in the picture or text that suggests this information.

● Then ask them to link word clues with picture clues by drawing lines between them. Can they explain why these clues are linked?

● The children should then answer the questions, providing evidence to support their answers, and ask their own inference question.

Comprehension

● **Photocopiable pages 70 and 71 'Pearls'**

● Hand out the photocopiable sheets. Ask the children to find clues to explain what is happening in the text and pictures.

● They should then read the questions and highlight clues from them to respond accurately.

What's on the CD-ROM

On the CD-ROM you will find:
● Printable versions of all three photocopiable pages.
● Answers to 'Making meaning from clues' and 'Pearls (2)'.
● Interactive version of 'Making meaning from clues'.

Making meaning from clues

■ Highlight the word clues in the text and link them to clues in the picture to explain what is happening. Then answer the questions.

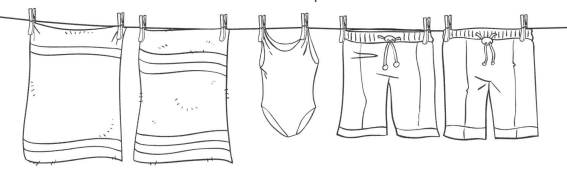

"I love a good day out!" he said.

"So do I!" she agreed with a deep sigh.

"What shall I do with all the leftover food, dear?" he asked.

"Bin it – I hate sand in my teeth. Hey, don't leave the snorkel and flippers there!" she snapped.

"My nose is sore, Mum."

"I don't know! I told you to put lotion on – but you wouldn't listen! Go and fetch the after-sun lotion."

1. Who went out for the day? Explain how you know.

_____

_____

2. Where had they been for the day? How do you know that?

_____

_____

3. What clues suggest Mum did join in when they were out? Why do you say that?

_____

_____

4. Your inference question:

_____

Your answer:

_____

Illustrations © 2009, JHS Studio/Beehive Illustration.

**Seeking evidence
from pictures and text**

Pearls (1)

Dad gave me a string of pearls for my birthday.
They aren't real pearls but they look real.
They came nested in deep, deep blue velvet
    in a hinged box with a silvery lid.
His sister had some like them when she was my age.
She was thrilled.
He thought I'd really like them.
I said I did.

I love the box.

Jean Little

Seeking evidence from pictures and text

Pearls (2)

1. What did the child value most about the gift? How do you know that?

_____

_____

2. Were pearls a special gift to give a girl when Dad was young? Explain how you know this.

_____

_____

3. Was the girl truthful with her dad about really liking the necklace? What clues tell you the answer?

_____

_____

4. Your question:

_____

_____

Your answer: How do you know that?

_____

_____

5. Your question:

_____

_____

Your answer: How do you know that?

_____

_____

Presenting evidence

Objective

To gather and present evidence that indicates a full understanding of the author's intention.

Background knowledge

This section shows the children how to assemble and present well-reasoned evidence from information to demonstrate how or why they know the answer to an inference question. It explains how good text detectives offer proof that clearly explains the author's or illustrator's hidden meaning and intention.

These activities show the children how to use the conjunction 'because' to elicit a full evidence-based answer to an inference question. This device helps them to link question key words to inferred text and picture clues.

It may be helpful to refer the children to Chapter 3, Section 2 (page 46) that explains how links are made between cause-and-effect clues.

Skills

Explain to the children that these activities will show them how to link question clues and text and pictures clues to give fully justified answers to inference questions.

● **Photocopiable page 73 'Choosing a cat to rehome'**

● Explain that in order to give a full answer to an inference question the children need to give a good reason for an answer. They need to say why or how they know the answer by offering proof that explains the implied meaning within the information they have read.

● To do this the children need to use the word 'because' to link the first part of their answer (using part of the question to guide them) to the second part that explains how they know.

● Hand out the photocopiable sheet and talk about the example given. Discuss how the images and the emboldened clues in the question and text are linked to give a full answer using the conjunction 'because'.

● Explain that 'because' is linked to cause and effect and is used to explain why something is happening or might happen.

● Taking note of the emboldened clues in the text, ask the children to give a full answer to each question using 'because'.

Comprehension

● **Photocopiable pages 74 and 75 'Bird box leaflet'**

● Hand out the photocopiable sheets. Ask the children to highlight the key word clues in the text.

● Once they have done this, ask them to give fully justified answers to the questions and generate and answer their own question.

What's on the CD-ROM

On the CD-ROM you will find:
● Printable versions of all three photocopiable pages.
● Answers to 'Choosing a cat to rehome' and 'Bird box leaflet (2)'.
● Interactive version of 'Choosing a cat to rehome'.

Presenting evidence

Choosing a cat to rehome

■ Read the text below. Use the text to answer the questions, giving reasons for your answer. Remember to use **because**. The first one has been done for you.

1. Shy cats: Timid cats tend to go **unnoticed**, yet they can be the most loyal of pets once you have gained their trust. They often **hide away** when visitors first come to a rescue centre, but once they are home with you, they reward your patience and kindness with great affection.

Example:
Question: Why do timid cats tend to go unnoticed when people first visit rescue centres to choose a pet?
Answer: Timid cats tend to go unnoticed when people first visit rescue centres to choose a pet **because** they are shy and **often hide away**.

2. Senior cats: Some people **prefer to adopt an older cat**. Mature cats usually settle into a new home quickly and are very house-trained and undemanding!

Question: Why do some people choose to adopt senior cats? Give two reasons.
Answer: Some people choose to adopt senior cats because

_____

_____

3. Black cats, and black and white cats: People often **pass by these cats** in favour of others who are more colourful. Please give a black and white cat or a 'lucky black cat' a chance!

Question: Do people prefer black cats? How do you know that?

Answer: _____

_____

Illustrations © 2009, JHS Studio/Beehive Illustration.

Name:

Bird box leaflet (1)

Join the BBC Nest Box Challenge by putting up a box in your garden, school or workplace. Register your box on our website and tell us if any birds move in! This will help the British Trust for Ornithology's survey about wild birds.

Here are my top tips to get you started:

1. You can make your own nest box or buy a BTO approved one from your local garden centre.

2. Check the wooden box comes from a sustainable source (look for the FSC logo) and that it has drainage at the bottom. Make sure the lid is secure so magpies and squirrels can't get in.

3. Put your box up where it is sheltered from the wind, rain and strong sunlight. Avoid 'busy' areas eg near bird feeders or right next to windows.

4. Other animals may try to get in to eat eggs or young chicks, so securely fasten your box to a wall or tree.

5. Find out which boxes suit which birds and much more at bbc.co.uk/breathingplaces, or ask for advice at your local library.

Best wishes,

Chris Packham

PS: Watch *Nature's Calendar* on BBC Two for more tips!

breathing places

BBC Nest Box Challenge is part of BBC Breathing Places, inspiring thousands of people to get involved with Nature.

bbc.co.uk/breathingplaces

This postcard has been printed on 100% recycled paper produced from de-inked post consumer waste and has been printed using vegetable-based inks. Please recycle.

Give a bird a home

Take part in the BBC Nest Box Challenge

BTO

NATIONAL NEST BOX WEEK

The Nest Box Challenge is led by BBC Local Radio during Breathing Places is working with National Nest Box Week which is organised by the BTO and sponsored by Jacobi Jayne & Co.

breathing places   **bbc.co.uk/breathingplaces**

Text and illustrations © 2007, BBC.

Bird box leaflet (2)

1. Is this leaflet designed to encourage young people to look after wild birds in this country? Explain how you know that.

_____

_____

_____

2. Are nesting birds safe from other birds and animals in the wooden box when the lid is on tightly? How do you know that?

_____

_____

_____

3. Explain why it is important that your wooden box is protected from the weather when it is put up.

_____

_____

_____

4. Your question: _____

_____

Your answer: How do you know that?

_____

_____

5. Your question: _____

_____

Your answer: How do you know that?

_____

_____

Inference questions

Objective

To gather, organise and classify inferred information to formulate questions and answers from text.

Background knowledge

This section shows the children how to gather and organise complex inference clues to generate their own questions and answers from text. These invaluable skills will help them to demonstrate an understanding of the author's intention from several perspectives, and encourage them to search the text for more multi-faceted answers. With practice they will soon be able to question and respond by making links with a variety of key word clues in different parts of the text. They will see for themselves how there is often more than one correct answer to an inference question. As long as the evidence presented justifies the answer to a question, then it is acceptable.

These essential skills encourage the children to think for themselves and help them to investigate and question, make reasoned deductions and present evidence with confidence that will make an impact on their learning across the curriculum.

Skills

Explain to the children that these activities will show them how to find inference clues that will help them to ask and answer their own questions about story or non-fiction text.

● **Photocopiable page 77 'Settling into our new home'**
   ● Remind the children that inference questions ask readers to solve clues from information that is suggested in the text. They also need to justify their answers, using evidence that may be found in different parts of the text.

● Hand out the photocopiable sheet and read the passage aloud to the children. Ask them to listen out for clues that imply something, for example: 'servant' – this is not a story about a modern couple, 'landlord' – the couple do not own the house.
● Ask the children to circle key word clues given on the page and search for other implied words and phrases, such as: servant: 'going to front door/taken from her work'; landlord: 'took £2 off the rent'.
● Tell the children to read the example question. Together, talk about the answer provided. Point out how the clues link the question to the text, and explain how the questions on the page check the readers' understanding of the author's meaning.
● Now ask the children to answer the question at the foot of the page, using the second set of key word clues.
● Finally, invite the children to generate their own questions from clues and information in the text.

Comprehension

● **Photocopiable pages 78 and 79 'Ways to live forever'**
   ● Hand out the photocopiable sheets. Ask the children to highlight the key information clues in the text.
   ● Tell them to answer the first two questions and then generate and answer their own questions.

What's on the CD-ROM

On the CD-ROM you will find:
● Printable versions of all three photocopiable pages.
● Answers to 'Settling into our new home' and 'Ways to live forever (2)'.
● Interactive version of 'Settling into our new home'.

Inference questions

Settling into our new home

■ Read the text and look at the example question. Answer the second question using the key word clues to help you. Write some of your own questions and answers on a separate sheet.

My dear wife Carrie and I have just been **a week in our new house**, 'The Laurels', Brickfield Terrace, Holloway – a nice six-roomed residence, not counting basement, with a front breakfast-parlour. We have a little front garden; and there is a flight of ten steps up to the front door, which, by the by, we keep locked with the chain up. Cummings, Gowing and our other intimate friends always come to the little side entrance, which saves **the servant** the **trouble** of going up to the **front door**, thereby **taking her from her work.** We have a nice little back garden which runs down to the railway. We were rather afraid of the **noise of the trains** at first, but the landlord said we should not notice them after a bit, and took £2 off the rent. He was certainly right; and beyond the **cracking of the garden wall** at the bottom, we have suffered no inconvenience.

(from *The Diary of a Nobody* by George and Weedon Grossmith)

Key word clues:	a week in our new house the servant trouble front door taking her from her work noise of the trains cracking of the garden wall

1. Did the author and his wife have **any problems to solve** in their new home over the **first week**? Explain how you know that.

Yes, the author and his wife had to solve some problems in the first week because they had to ask their friends to come to the little side entrance to save the servant the trouble of going up to the front door and taking her from her work. They also noticed the noise of the trains at first and there was a crack in the garden wall.

Key word clues:	our new house landlord rent

2. Do Carrie and her husband own their new house? How do you know that?

_____

_____

Illustrations © 2009, JHS Studio/Beehive Illustration.

Inference questions

Ways to live forever (1)

Questions nobody answers no. 1: How do you know that you've died?

9th January

Today we had school again. I told Mrs Willis I was going to write a book.

"It's about me," I said. "But also it's a scientific inquiry. I've done loads." And I showed her my first 'Questions Nobody Answers'.

"Very commendable," she said. "How exactly are you going to find the answers to these things?"

"I'm going to look them up on the Internet," I said.

You can find out anything on the Internet.

Mrs Willis let me and Felix look up how you know that you've died today. We had to bring Dad's laptop down from the study, because Felix has a wheelchair at the moment. When I first met him he was only in it some of the time, but he's almost always in it now. He can walk really. He just likes having people wait on him.

We started with www.ask.com and ended up with this website on near-death experiences. A near-death experience is when someone almost dies but changes their mind at the last minute and comes back. The website said this happens to five per cent of adults in America.

"So they *say*," said Felix.

All sorts of things happened to these people, according to the website. They went down dark tunnels. They saw bright lights and angels. Sometimes they floated over their body and saw their doctors talking about them or giving them electric shocks. It was exactly the sort of science I want to do. I thought it was brilliant. Felix didn't.

"It's not real," he said. "How can everyone see angels? What about serial killers?"

Text © 2008, Sally Nicholls.

Inference questions

Ways to live forever (2)

| Internet | website | dark tunnels | bright lights | floated over their body |
| angels | doctors talking about them | giving them electric shocks |

1. Did the main character find the answer to the question? Explain how you know.

_____

_____

| So they _say_ | I thought it was brilliant | Felix didn't | it's not real |
| how can everyone see angels | serial killers |

2. Does Felix believe that 5 per cent of adult Americans have had a near-death experience? How do you know that?

_____

_____

3. Your inference question:

_____

_____

Your answer:

_____

_____

4. Your inference question:

_____

_____

Your answer:

_____

_____

Chapter 5
Clarification

Introduction

This chapter helps children make sense of what they read by showing them how to resolve difficulties with unfamiliar words, images and concepts such as 'time frames'. They are taught explicitly how to combine prior knowledge and contextual clues to elicit meaning from the figurative writing devices that authors use.

It also teach children how to identify synonyms and antonyms, and to skim and scan for word and picture clues as evidence to justify answers to questions with ease and accuracy.

Poster notes

The text patrol (page 81)

This poster shows how a combination of prior knowledge and context clues helps children to make sense of unknown words. It shows them how to isolate what they know of a difficult word and fathom its meaning from their understanding of the words around it.

They are shown how PC Code-Breaker solves difficult words by pacing back over the sentence to gain the gist of the author's meaning, and by breaking down the difficult word into small parts. Finally, he checks that the meaning he has in his head fits the sense of the sentence and the context of the passage he is reading.

In this chapter

	About the section	About the comprehension
Understanding time in storytelling page 82	Children make sense of an unknown concept to reveal meaning.	Children look for picture and word clues to explain the time and location shifts in Anthony Horowitz's *Stormbreaker*™.
Unfamiliar words page 86	Children identify the meaning of unknown words from contextual clues.	Children seek picture and word clues to explain meaning of unfamiliar vocabulary in *Castle Diary* by Richard Platt.
Similes and metaphors page 90	Children identify figurative language.	Children seek meaning for similes and metaphors in *Keeper* by Mal Peet.
Skimming and scanning for similar and opposite meanings page 94	Children build on skimming and scanning to link synonym or antonym clues in text and questions.	Children answer inference questions about an extract from *Carrie's War* by Nina Bawden.

Clarification

The text patrol

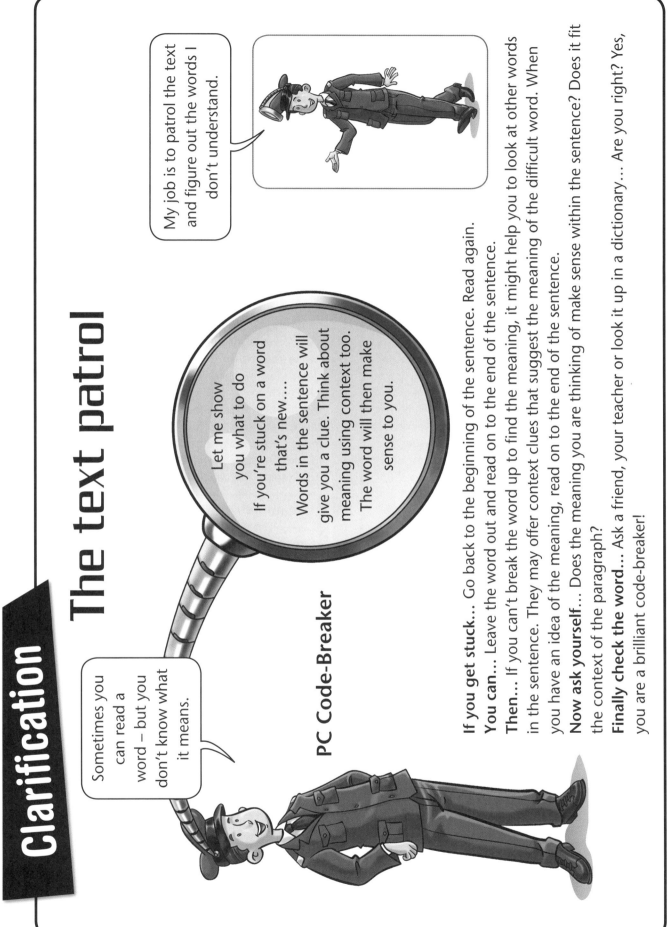

My job is to patrol the text and figure out the words I don't understand.

Let me show you what to do If you're stuck on a word that's new…. Words in the sentence will give you a clue. Think about meaning using context too. The word will then make sense to you.

PC Code-Breaker

Sometimes you can read a word – but you don't know what it means.

If you get stuck… Go back to the beginning of the sentence. Read again.
You can… Leave the word out and read on to the end of the sentence.
Then… If you can't break the word up to find the meaning, it might help you to look at other words in the sentence. They may offer context clues that suggest the meaning of the difficult word. When you have an idea of the meaning, read on to the end of the sentence.
Now ask yourself… Does the meaning you are thinking of make sense within the sentence? Does it fit the context of the paragraph?
Finally check the word… Ask a friend, your teacher or look it up in a dictionary… Are you right? Yes, you are a brilliant code-breaker!

Illustrations © 2009, JHS Studio/Beehive Illustration.

Understanding time in storytelling

Objective

Objective

To understand how authors use interchanging time sequences to tell a story.

Background knowledge

This section explains how authors indicate when there is a change in time by using writing devices that cover multiple events from the past, future or present to explain the conflicts and outcomes for characters in the present.

In real life, people experience time in a linear way where the 'now' point is ongoing. Similarly, as children read, they expect the 'now' to move forward continuously. So for authors to take their reader to another time or location successfully, they provide clues that link together – and the tense changes. They give the reader clues (such as 'meanwhile') that suggest that several events are still going on in the present. Or an author might simply tell us the location of an event that is happening at the same time. The author might use other clues (like future or past tense) to show the reader that the story has moved backwards or forwards in time.

Skills

Tell the children that these activities will help them to understand how to interpret different time-frame sequences in a story.

- **Photocopiable page 83 'Time guide'**
  - Explain that authors use time to transport their readers to another moment in time or location to explain conflicts and outcomes for characters within a story.

- Authors use different tenses and clues such as 'earlier' and 'later' to show when parts of the story are occurring at different times. They also refer to events in different locations that are set in the same time, using cues such as 'meanwhile' to indicate this.
- Hand out the photocopiable sheet. Ask the children to read the information in the time guide and to imagine they are film directors who are filming 'Goldilocks' in three different locations.
- Explain that locations are given in the text and that the arrows on the guide indicate movement between past, present and future sequences in the story. Ask the children, working in groups, to discuss where 'meanwhile', 'earlier' and 'later' should go to clarify what is happening in the story. Tell them to label each box with the correct time clue.
- Ask them to retell the story to their partner to check that it makes sense. Then plan a story time frame using the organiser provided. Suggest story themes that have overlapping times and locations (for example, *Cinderella*).

Comprehension

- **Photocopiable pages 84 and 85 'Stormbreaker™'**
  - Hand out the photocopiable sheets. Ask the children to read the text and to study the images.
  - Tell them to look for time and location cues in the pictures and dialogue that help to identify the characters involved. Then ask them to answer the comprehension questions on the second sheet.

 **What's on the CD-ROM**

On the CD-ROM you will find:
- Printable versions of all three photocopiable pages.
- Answers to 'Time guide' and 'Stormbreaker™ (2)'.
- Interactive version of 'Time guide'.

Name:

Time guide

■ Look at the time frame below. The box in the centre is the main event which is happening in the present. The arrows show the relationship with that time. Write **earlier**, **later** or **meanwhile** on each line to show when the event is happening compared to the present event.

■ Create your own time frame for a story of your choosing.

Location

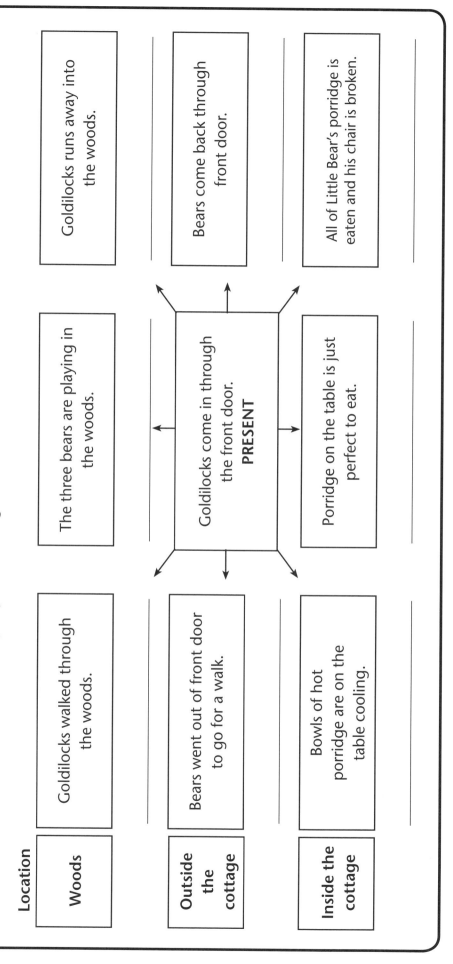

Location		
Woods	Goldilocks walked through the woods.	The three bears are playing in the woods.	Goldilocks runs away into the woods.
		Goldilocks come in through the front door. **PRESENT**	Bears come back through front door.
Outside the cottage	Bears went out of front door to go for a walk.	Porridge on the table is just perfect to eat.	All of Little Bear's porridge is eaten and his chair is broken.
Inside the cottage	Bowls of hot porridge are on the table cooling.		

Name:

Stormbreaker™ (1)

Text and illustration © 2006, Walker Books.

PHOTOCOPIABLE

Understanding time in storytelling

Stormbreaker™ (2)

1. Explain why authors use different times and locations to tell a story.

2. Where does Alex's uncle work? How do you know that?

3. From the evidence in the story, do you think Alex's uncle has 'a really boring job'? Explain why you say that.

4. Would you choose 'earlier', 'meanwhile' or 'later' to explain the time difference in the story? Explain your reason.

5. Your clarification question:

   Your answer:

SCHOLASTIC
www.scholastic.co.uk   **PHOTOCOPIABLE**   Scholastic Literacy Skills
Comprehension: Year 5   **85**

Unfamiliar words

To make sense of unfamiliar words and expressions, using contextual clues and prior knowledge to seek meaning.

Background knowledge

This section shows the children how to solve unfamiliar and outdated language from diary accounts to support their understanding of historical text. Diary entries are a form of non-fiction writing that is a personal account of an individual's everyday experiences. They are mostly written in the past tense, are related to events in chronological order and use paragraphs for changes of time, event and action.

Diary entries written generations ago will be full of unfamiliar words and expressions of the time, and may seem incomprehensible at first to children. However, although these words may appear strange at first, they can often be understood by drawing on the meaning of more familiar words and terms in the same sentence or nearby text.

These skills help children to combine their prior knowledge, prediction and interpretation skills to make sense out of confusion as they read.

Skills

Tell the children that these activities will help them to define the meaning of unknown words and expressions from context clues.

- **Photocopiable page 87 'Blagging it'**
  - Explain that diaries are used to record the author's daily experiences. They are a form of non-fiction writing that often offers a fascinating account of people's lives in very different times. However, because the language may be unfamiliar and difficult to understand, the children need to clarify meanings as they go along.

- Explain that old-fashioned words and expressions can often be broken into parts to reveal smaller words that the children know (for example, 'chimney-glass'). Tell them that these word parts often uncover the meaning of the whole word as soon as they are linked to contextual clues.
- Hand out the photocopiable sheet and ask the children to read the two passages.
- They can complete the sheet in two ways – either in pairs, discussing the possible definition, or they can play the game 'Blagging it' in teams of three or four players (see below).
- For 'Blagging it', give each team one of the words (or phrases) identified in bold in the text extracts. Ask the teams to discuss and predict the meaning of their word from parts they already understand or from context clues in the passage. Explain that each team will take turns to provide three definitions of their word – two will be 'blags' or 'bluffs', the other definition will be correct. Each team will choose a definition and say why they think it is correct. Remind the children that the definition must make sense within the context of the passage.

Comprehension

- **Photocopiable pages 88 and 89 'Castle diary'**
  - Hand out the photocopiable sheets. Explain to the children that these are two diary entries from a castle inhabitant. Tell them to read the entries.
  - Ask the children to identify the difficult words in the text and to seek meaning from clues within the word and context clues in order to answer the questions. They can then generate their own questions about the passage.

 **What's on the CD-ROM**

On the CD-ROM you will find:
- Printable versions of all three photocopiable pages.
- Answers to 'Blagging it' and 'Castle diary (2)'.
- Interactive version of 'Blagging it' and 'Castle diary'.

Unfamiliar words

Blagging it

■ Read the text extracts below (from *The Diary of a Nobody* by George and Weedon Grossmith). Try to work out the definitions to the words in bold.

■ You could play the game of 'Blagging it' where teams invent three definitions of a word, but only one is correct and the other team has to guess which one it is.

August 29, 1892

Mrs James is making a positive fool of Carrie. Carrie appeared in a new dress like a **smock-frock**. She said 'smocking' was **all the rage**. I replied it put me in a rage. She also had on a hat as big as a kitchen **coal-scuttle**, and the same shape.

■ Write definitions for each of these words on the lines provided.

smock-frock _____

all the rage _____

coal-scuttle _____

May 7, 1892

The last time it was the greengrocer's boy, who, not seeing it was me, for Sarah had not lighted the gas, pushed into my hands two cabbages and half a dozen coal-blocks. I indignantly threw them on the ground, and felt so annoyed that I so far forgot myself as to **box the boy's ears**. He went away crying, and said he should **summons** me, a thing I would not have happen for the world. In the dark, I stepped on a piece of the cabbage, which brought me down on the **flags** all of a heap. For a moment I was stunned, but when I recovered I crawled upstairs into the drawing room and on looking into the **chimney-glass** discovered that my chin was bleeding, my shirt smeared with the coal-blocks, and my left trouser torn at the knee.

■ Write definitions for each of these words on the lines provided.

box the boy's ears _____

summons _____

flags _____

chimney-glass _____

Illustrations © 2009, JHS Studio/Beehive Illustration.

Name:

Unfamiliar words

Castle diary (1)

June 13th, Wednesday
The garderobes all reek. When I have need of them I rush nimbly, clutching my nose. I let fall my hose and pray that relief will be quick. This forenoon when I sat upon the wooden seat, out from under it flew a black fly so fat that at first I took it to be a wren.

June 15th, Friday
This day the GONG-FARMER came from the village to work below the South Wall. On this side of the castle the garderobes empty down chutes into the moat. But because there has been no rain, the moat is sluggish in its flow and everything that falls from the chutes stays where it drops. The Gong-Farmer must clear not only these piles but others besides, for elsewhere in the castle the garderobes empty into pits which must be cleaned to keep them sweet.

One of the garderobe chutes is blocked and the Gong-Farmer must reach up inside this slimy pipe to unclog it. I would not do his job for all the King's gold.

A humming black cloud hangs always above a Gong-Farmer's head. Nose warns of his approach long before eyes espy him, and all ears are alert to the squeaking of his stinking cart.

Text © 1999, Richard Platt; illustration © 1999, Chris Riddell.

Unfamiliar words

Castle diary (2)

1. What do you think 'garderobes' are? What evidence do you have for saying this?

_____

_____

_____

2. Is the author writing about his visit to the garderobes in the morning or afternoon of 13th June? Explain how you know that.

_____

_____

_____

3. Do you think the Gong-Farmer's job was made easier in the hot dry summer months? Why do you say that?

_____

_____

_____

4. Explain what you think the author means when he says 'a humming black cloud hangs always above a Gong-Farmer's head'.

_____

_____

5. Your vocabulary question:

_____

_____

Your answer:

_____

_____

Similes and metaphors

Objective

To be able to identify and understand metaphor within text.

Background knowledge

This section focuses on how to generate similes which are a simple form of metaphor. Similes and metaphors are language devices which use comparison.

A simile likens something to something else using 'as' or 'like'. For example, if someone had a very red face, we might say *His face was as red as a tomato* or *He sped off like a rocket*.

A metaphor is very similar to a simile but does not use 'as' or 'like'. For example, *She had a very sunny personality* is a metaphor, while *Her personality was as bright as the sun* would be a simile.

Skills

This activity will show the children how to identify and generate similes and metaphors within text.

- **Photocopiable page 91 'Similes and metaphors'**
  - Explain that a simile describes something by comparing it to something else using 'as' or 'like'. For example, *His face was as red as a tomato* or *She slept like a baby*.
  - Tell the children that metaphors are like similes but they do not use 'as' or 'like' to make a comparison – instead they say something *is* something else, such as *My best friend is a rock to me*.
  - Ask the class to think of examples of similes and metaphors that are used all the time.

- Hand out the photocopiable sheet. Ask the children to read the examples given and to take each pair of opposite words (antonyms) – *strong/weak, white/black, fast/slow, smooth/rough* – and generate as many connected words as they can think of, before they complete the similes. For example, ask the children to write *as strong as* on one side of a separate sheet of paper and surround it with other words that come to mind, such as *iron, steel, wrestler, boxer, lion, tough, burly, grizzly bear, ox*. Ask them to then write *weak* on the other side of their sheet of paper and do the same.
- Suggest that the children now use some of these words to help them to complete the similes in the first part of the photocopiable sheet.
- Once they have done this, ask them to think of some more similes that they can use to complete the second section.
- Finally, ask the children to explain the meaning of the metaphors in the last section of the sheet.

Comprehension

- **Photocopiable pages 92 and 93 'Keeper'**
  - Hand out copies of the photocopiable sheets. Ask the children to read the text and discuss it with them. Ask them to highlight the metaphors and similes in the passage.
  - They should then answer the questions on the second sheet before generating and answering their own question.

 What's on the CD-ROM

On the CD-ROM you will find:
- Printable versions of all three photocopiable pages.
- Answers to 'Keeper (2)'.
- Interactive versions of 'Similes and metaphors' and 'Keeper'.

Similes and metaphors

Similes and metaphors

■ Think of some suitable words to complete the similes below.

As strong as _____

As weak as _____

As white as _____

The night was black like _____

She was fast like _____

As slow as _____

The pebble was as smooth as _____

It felt rough like _____

■ Now complete the following sentences, using suitable similes.

The moon rose in the sky like _____

The roots of the tree were like _____

Water cascaded down the waterfall like _____

Fireworks exploded into the sky like _____

The silence was like _____

■ Explain the meaning of the following metaphors.

He fixed her with an icy stare. _____

_____

Her voice is beginning to grate on me. _____

_____

He was a shady character. _____

_____

You could cut the atmosphere with a knife. _____

_____

Name:

Keeper (1)

I knew every inch of the path, of course, and all its tricks – the places where it hid itself, pretended to fade away, the places where the forest stretched its fingers out to lash at your eyes, where roots snaked out to trip you up. But I had never gone in there at night before, and I had never run so desperately towards the clearing. Here and there tiny splashes of silver light lay on the forest floor like coins, and now and again I caught a glimpse of the fat-faced moon sliding through the canopy of branches way above me.

I was shaking, and soaked with sweat, when I stumbled into the clearing. I put my hands on my knees and dragged the air, always sharper and cleaner here, into my lungs. The clearing was drenched in cold light. The moon had come to a stop overhead. Everything was divided into just two colours: brilliant silver and an inky blue-black. The silence was like something solid you could lean against, and rest, and recover from miracles.

I did not expect the Keeper to be there. Whatever and whoever he was, he seemed to depend on daylight. I was quite sure he would not materialize at night. When my breathing had steadied, I straightened up.

He was standing in the goalmouth, his back against the right post, arms folded over his chest, staring at the ground. No football. My heart lurched like a truck going over a rut in the road. It was as hard as it had ever been to walk towards him. I stopped at the penalty spot.

"It has happened, then," he said. It was not a question. So I didn't answer.

Similes and metaphors

Keeper (2)

1. Was the main character used to walking along the path at any time of the day? How do you know that?

_____

_____

_____

2. Give an example of a simile from the passage. Explain what it means in the context of the passage.

_____

_____

_____

3. How does the author use metaphor to suggest the forest was in some way alive?

_____

_____

4. Is there a sharp contrast between light and dark in the forest? Explain how you know this.

_____

_____

5. What do you think the author means when he compares the silence to something you can lean against?

_____

_____

6. Your question:

_____

Your answer:

_____

Skimming and scanning for similar and opposite meanings

Objectives

To learn how to skim and scan for similar and opposite meanings within text and pictures that link to question key clues. To infer from these clues to answer questions and support deduction.

Background knowledge

The activities in this section show the children how to skim and scan for synonyms and antonyms in text. They learn how to locate key words in a question and search for word clues that have similar or opposite meanings. Skimming and scanning for these clues enables children to answer and generate their own inference questions with greater ease and to respond to questions accurately and appropriately.

Searching for and identifying synonyms and antonyms also helps children to enlarge their understanding of word meanings within context; it also serves to extend their vocabulary and stimulate prediction and deduction.

Skills

These activities show the children how to answer inference questions accurately by finding similar and opposite key clues in text and images to match the word clues in the questions.

- **Photocopiable page 95 'Oliver Twist'**
  - Explain that many inference questions need you to skim and scan information for similar and opposite meanings in order to answer word clues in the questions.
  - Hand out the photocopiable sheet. Read the passage with the children and discuss the vocabulary within the text.

- Ask them to re-read the passage in pairs and to think about each of the emboldened words in context. What other word would make sense in place of each word?
- Tell the children to look at the first list of words. Each links to words in the text. Ask them to skim and scan the text and, using coloured pens, circle the word that is similar in meaning to the word listed, explaining why to their partner.
- Ask the children to repeat this exercise with the second list of words. They must focus on finding the opposite meanings to these in the emboldened words and circle them in a different-coloured pen.
- Finally, ask the children to read the questions at the bottom of the page and to answer them, using the circled words in the text to help them.

Comprehension

- **Photocopiable pages 96 and 97 'Carrie's war'**
  - Hand out the photocopiable sheets and ask the children to read the text.
  - Tell them to read the questions on the second photocopiable sheet and to highlight any key words that link to the text before they answer the questions.

What's on the CD-ROM

On the CD-ROM you will find:
- Printable versions of all three photocopiable pages.
- Answers to 'Oliver Twist' and 'Carrie's war (2)'.
- Interactive versions of 'Oliver Twist' and 'Carrie's war'.

Skimming and scanning for similar and opposite meanings

Oliver Twist

■ Look at the words in bold. Can you think of different words you could use instead of them?

The boy who addressed this **inquiry** to the young **wayfarer** was about his own age, but one of the **queerest-looking** boys that Oliver had ever seen. He was a snub-nosed, flat-browed, common-faced boy enough, and as **dirty** a **juvenile** as one would wish to see; but he had about him all the airs and manners of a man. He was **short** of his age, with rather bow legs, and little, **sharp, ugly** eyes. His hat was stuck on the top of his head so **lightly**, that it threatened to fall off every moment – and would have done so, very often, if the wearer had not had a knack of every now and then giving his head a sudden twitch, which brought it back to its old place again. He wore a man's coat, which reached nearly to his heels. He had turned the cuffs **back**, half way up his arm, to get his hands out of the sleeves: apparently with the ultimate view of **thrusting** them into the pockets of his corduroy trousers, for there he kept them.

    He was, altogether, as roistering and **swaggering** a young gentleman as ever stood four feet six, or something less, in his bluchers.

(From *Oliver Twist* by Charles Dickens)

■ Skim and scan the passage to find synonyms (similar words) in the text to the following words.

question	traveller	youth	hideous	plunging	strutting

■ Skim and scan the poem to find antonyms (opposite words) in the text to the following words.

clean	tall	ordinary-looking	blunt	heavily	forward

■ Discuss the answers to these questions with a partner. Remember to explain how you know.

1. Did the boy ask the young traveller a question?
2. Was the boy a clean, ordinary-looking youth?
3. Did the boy's hat sit heavily on his head?
4. Did he push his cuffs forward to plunge his hands into his pockets?

Illustration © 2009, JHS Studio/Beehive Illustration.

Name:

Carrie's war (1)

Carrie had often dreamed about coming back. In her dreams she was twelve years old again; short, scratched legs in red socks and scuffed, brown sandals, walking along the narrow, dirt path at the side of the railway line to where it plunged down, off the high ridge, through the Druid's Grove. The yew trees in the Grove were dark green and so old that they had grown twisted and lumpy, like arthritic fingers. And in Carrie's dream, the fingers reached out for her, plucking at her hair and her skirt as she ran. She was always running by the end of this dream, running away from the house, uphill towards the railway line.

But when she did come back, with her own children, the railway line had been closed. The sleepers had been taken up and the flat, stony top of the ridge was so overgrown with blackberries and wild rose and hazelnut bushes that it was like pushing through a forgotten forest in a fairy tale. The tangled wood round Sleeping Beauty's castle. Pulling off the sticky brambles that clung to her jeans, Carrie's children said, "No one's been here for hundreds of years…"

"Not hundreds, *thousands*…"

"A hundred, thousand years. A million, billion, trillion…"

"Only about thirty," Carrie said. She spoke as if this was no time at all. "*I* was here, with Uncle Nick, thirty years ago. During the war – when England was at war with Germany. The Government sent the children out of the cities so they shouldn't be bombed. We weren't told where we were going. Just told to turn up at our schools with a packed lunch and a change of clothes, then we went to the station with our teachers. There were whole train-loads of children sent away like that…"

"Without their mummies?" the little ones said. "Without their *dads*?"

"Oh, quite alone," Carrie said. "I was eleven when we first came here. And Uncle Nick was going on ten."

Uncle Nick was old. He had been old for years and grown so fat in the stomach that he puffed when he stooped. The thought of him being ten years old made the children want to giggle but they bit the giggles back. Their mother was looking so strange: eyes half closed and dreaming. They looked at her pale, dreaming face and said nothing.

Text © 1973, Nina Bawden.

Carrie's war (2)

1. Read the passage. Find words in the passage that have similar meaning to these words and write them on the line.

returning _____

pulling at _____

escaping _____

2. Read the passage then find a word from it that means the opposite to these words in the text and write them on the line.

opened _____

uneven _____

remembered _____

3. Does the author make a comparison between the yew trees and old age? Explain how she does this.

_____

_____

_____

4. Does the author move the story backwards and forwards in time? Explain why you say this.

_____

_____

5. Was young Carrie sent away to the country for her own safety? How do you know?

_____

_____

6. Your question (using a synonym or antonym):

_____

Your answer:

_____

Chapter 6

Evaluation

This chapter builds on what the children already know about generating literal and inference questions. Evaluation refers here to personal interpretation of story characters that links to the author's viewpoint, rather than the term that is generally used to mean a critical appraisal of text by the reader. It is generally a question-type that children enjoy because it asks them to explain what they think the characters' feelings, thoughts and actions might be based on, using their own experience and understanding of the world. They also like evaluation questions because – as long as they justify their answers from the text and pictures – any answer is valid. In addition, evaluation questioning develops empathy and evidence-based reasoning to support personal opinion and debate.

Poster notes

Are you a private detective? (page 99)
The 'private detective' analogy explains how to make meaning of words and images by using a combination of all the comprehension skills: literal, prediction, clarification and inference. This poster supports children's understanding of evaluation and introduces them to the private detectives who are the highest-ranking officers of the Literacy Police Force. Reference to 'private' reminds the children that evaluation detective work also asks them to add personal experiences and knowledge to help them give reasoned answers to questions about the characters' feelings, actions and thoughts that the author might agree with.

In this chapter

	About the section	About the comprehension
Characters' feelings and actions page 100	Children interpret facial expressions and body language.	Children generate and answer questions based on *When Jessie Came Across the Sea* by Amy Hest.
What you think and feel page 104	Children use personal experience and evidence from text and images to support evaluative reasoning.	Children focus on a passage from *Millions* by Frank Cottrell Boyce looking at the difference between literal, inference and evaluation questions.
Fact, opinion and evaluation page 108	Children identify evaluation clues to separate fact from opinion.	Children use *Lovely Grub* by Elspeth Graham to distinguish between fact and opinion to ask and answer evaluation questions.
Evaluation questions page 112	Children link evaluative key words in text and images to ask and answer questions about a characters' feelings, actions and thoughts.	Children study the poem 'Chips' by Stanley Cook using their own experience and knowledge to justify answers about characters' feelings/thoughts.

Evaluation

ARE YOU A PRIVATE DETECTIVE?

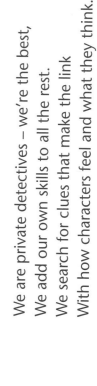

We tell you what **we think** is happening and **why** from our own experience and from the evidence on the page....

We are private detectives – we're the best,
We add our own skills to all the rest.
We search for clues that make the link
With how characters feel and what they think.

Characters' feelings and actions

Objective

To draw on own experience to interpret characters' emotions and actions within pictures and text to explain what is happening or may happen next.

Background knowledge

Visual imagery draws powerful evaluation responses from children, especially when it connects with their personal world. Evaluation questioning requires the children to be private detectives and ask themselves: *What do I think about the characters' feelings and actions in relation to my own experience?* It asks them to uncover evidence to explain the characters' behaviour, and unfolding events in the story. Children are particularly able to identify with the characters when facial expressions and body language are described explicitly in text or illustrated in pictures. The emotions they express prompt children's empathy and invite them to make links to other clues on the page, to deduce what is happening and what may happen next in the story.

Skills

These activities help the children to recognise and interpret facial expressions and body language to explain the thinking and behaviour of characters within picture narrative.

- **Photocopiable page 101 'Feelings and actions'**
  - Ask the children to explain how they know when someone is feeling happy, sad, angry and so on.
  - Talk with them about how our facial expressions and behaviour communicate our feelings and thoughts to others.

- Explain that facial expressions and body language do not generally need words for us to understand and predict what people are feeling or why they are behaving in a certain way. We all recognise and share the emotions behind these expressions from time to time.
- Hand out the photocopiable sheet. Ask the children to look closely at the four picture boxes and captions. Explain that each box contains a scene where the characters' feelings and emotions are being described by their body language and facial expressions.
- Working in pairs, ask the children to discuss the pictures and captions, then to locate the clues that explain what the characters might be feeling and thinking.
- Once they have located the picture and text clues, ask them to say what they think is happening and what may happen next in the scene.

Comprehension

- **Photocopiable pages 102 and 103 'When Jessie came across the sea'**
  - Hand out the photocopiable sheets to the children. Ask them to read the text and look at the pictures, then discuss these with a partner.
  - As the children answer the questions, remind them that there is no 'wrong' answer for an evaluation question – all answers are acceptable as long as their explanations refer to the picture and text as well as their own experience and knowledge.

 What's on the CD-ROM

On the CD-ROM you will find:
- Printable versions of all three photocopiable pages.
- Answers to 'When Jessie came across the sea (2)'.
- Interactive version of 'Feelings and actions'.

Feelings and actions

■ Look at the four pictures below. What does the body language and expression on the faces tell you about how they are feeling and what might happen next?

Odd one out

Into deep waters

Cool dress!

Snap!

Illustration © 2009, JHS Studio/Beehive Illustration.

Name:

When Jessie came across the sea (1)

On a fine autumn day they sailed past the Statue of Liberty. America! No one swapped stories or argued. Babies hushed. Even the oldest passengers, and the most seasick, stood against the rail. America!

And there it was, New York City with those tall, tall buildings that touched the sky.

Grandmother! Jessie thought.

If only you could see what I see now!

Text © 1997, Amy Hest; illustrations © 1997, P.J. Lynch.

Characters' feelings and actions

When Jessie came across the sea (2)

1. Explain how you think Jessie is feeling in the picture. Why do you say that?

   _____

   _____

2. Why do you think all the passengers stood silently against the rail?

   _____

   _____

3. Why do you think Jessie was thinking about her grandmother at this time? Explain why you say that.

   _____

   _____

   _____

4. What do you think the children are feeling? Why do you say that?

   _____

   _____

   _____

5. Your 'do you think' question:

   _____

   Your answer:

   _____

   _____

6. Your 'do you think' question:

   _____

   Your answer:

   _____

   _____

What you think and feel

Objective

To understand that an evaluation question asks you to use your literal and inference skills, as well as personal experience, to think about a character's feelings or actions.

Background knowledge

This section shows the children how to tell the difference between literal, inference and evaluation information within text. It encourages them to draw on personal experience to identify with characters' attitudes and feelings and helps them to use this information to find evidence on the page to support their evaluative reasoning.

To enable children to identify the difference between literal, inference and evaluation clues within text, it is helpful for them to first talk through what they can literally see is happening on the page. Then they should look more closely for descriptive clues that hint at meaning. Finally, they need to look at the author's portrayal of the character (behaviour, facial expressions, dialogue) and ask themselves what they think the characters might be feeling or thinking from the descriptions given. This reference to their own experiences and prior knowledge helps them to identify with the characters and make sense of the events in the scene.

Skills

These activities help the children to recognise evaluation and to see the difference between literal, inference and evaluation clues and evidence within picture narrative.

● **Photocopiable page 105 'Looking for different clues'**

   ● Begin by asking the children to explain the differences between literal PC Page and the inference Text Detective.

   ● Revisit poster page 63 and discuss how the Text Detective searches for evidence beyond obvious

'who', 'what' and 'where' information to show how he uncovers the author's meaning.

   ● Then, using poster page 99 'Are you a private detective?', show the children how they are able to add to the Text Detective's evidence by using their own personal experience to explain what might be happening from the characters' perspective.

   ● Hand out the photocopiable sheet. Ask the children to read and discuss the text in pairs.

   ● Explain that each section of text on the photocopiable sheet reveals particular information for PC Page, the Text Detective and the Private Detectives to ask and answer questions.

   ● Explain that section 1 contains basic 'who', 'what' and 'where' story information. Section 2 contains inference clues that suggest what has happened, is happening and what might happen next in the story. Ask the children to circle these clues and discuss in pairs what they think is going on in the story.

   ● Next, tell them to circle and discuss the evaluation clues in section 3 that indicate what the characters might be feeling or thinking. How are they different from inference clues?

Comprehension

● **Photocopiable pages 106 and 107 'Millions'**

   ● Hand out the photocopiable sheets. Ask the children to read the text through carefully before attempting the questions.

   ● The children need to remember the difference between question types in order to answer them correctly. Remind them that evaluation answers must refer to the text as well as personal experience.

What's on the CD-ROM

On the CD-ROM you will find:
● Printable versions of all three photocopiable pages.
● Answers to 'Millions (2)'.
● Interactive versions of 'Looking for different clues' and 'Millions'.

What you think and feel

Looking for different clues

■ Circle clues in the text to help PC Page, the Text Detective and the Private Detectives gather literal, inference and evaluation information.

1. Who? What? Where? Right there!
The two boys felt they had been drifting forever. After the angry heat of the day the fresh breeze off the water was soothing. It gave Tom fresh hope.
"Hey Sam, look over there!" he cried.

2. Being a text detective: what is happening and what might happen next
The tiny vessel rocked dangerously as Tom jumped up, waving his arms frantically at a familiar black shape on the horizon.

"Over here!" he shouted.

"Watch out, Tom – mind the rods and tackle!" said Sam, snatching at them and grabbing his friend before they all went overboard. "Sit down! They can't see us, we're too far away."

"We could do with that missing oar now," lamented Sam.

3. Being a private detective: finding evidence
"You're right. What's the point?" said Tom, slumping back into the boat. "We are never going to get rescued."

"Why did I listen to you?" Sam said, spitting the words out. "You said the outboard motor worked. You said 'we'll catch buckets of fish and be home in time for tea.' Now look at us!" Tears pricked his eyes. "...starving, thirsty, cold and miles from anywhere!"

The pair fell into a brooding silence, then finally into an exhausted sleep as the twilight faded into darkness.

Suddenly, flashing lights and whirring filled the sky and jolted them awake. Tom grabbed the torch in his pocket and shone it into the sky.

Private Detective

Private Detective

"It's a helicopter, Sam – they've come to get us!" he yelled. "We're going to be alright!"

Illustration © 2009, JHS Studio/Beehive Illustration.

Name:

Millions (1)

For a while we just looked at it. Then Anthony picked up a thousand pounds and put it crossways on top of another thousand. Then he picked up another and put it crossways on top of that. Then I picked up a pile and put that on top of the other three. Then Anthony. Then me, and on and on building a tower of cash. We got it almost as tall as me before it fell over. Then we both started laughing.

That was the first time we played Cash Jenga. We played it every night for the next week. The highest we ever got was Anthony's eyebrows. But that first time was the best, when it just sort of invented itself out of our excitement.

Cash Jenga is a great game if you can afford it.

We were late for school, but somehow it didn't matter. Whenever we saw each other in the playground or in the corridor, we just grinned. Having a secret is like having a pair of wings tucked in under your blazer. I gave Barry my Pringles (barbecue flavour) without being asked. I just handed them to him while we were lining up at the end of Small Play. I said "Enjoy." He looked a bit surprised.

On the way home we stopped at the shop and Anthony bought a bottle of Sunny Delight the size of an oxygen tank. He saw me looking at it and said to the man, "Make it a double."

While the man was getting my bottle, a girl from Anthony's class – the one with the nice corn rows in her hair – came in and Anthony said, "Make it three and have something for yourself." And he gave a tenner to the man and the bottle to the girl. Just as he was handing it to her, Barry came in and went "Ooooohooo, you love her! You brought her Sunny Delight."

"Why shouldn't I buy her Sunny Delight?"

"Why shouldn't you buy *me* Sunny Delight?"

"All right, then, I will."

Text © 2004, Frank Cottrell Boyce; illustration © 2009, JHS Studio/Beehive Illustration.

What you think and feel

Millions (2)

1. What did Anthony buy that was the size of an oxygen tank?

2. Do you have to be rich to play Cash Jenga? How do you know that?

3. How do you think the boys felt about having so much money? What are the clues that tell you this?

4. Explain what you think the author means when he says 'a secret is like having a pair of wings under your blazer'.

5. Do you think the man in the shop thought Anthony was behaving normally? Why do you say that?

6. Your literal question:

   Your answer:

7. Your inference question:

   Your answer:

8. Your evaluation question:

   Your answer:

Fact, opinion and evaluation

Objective

To distinguish between literal facts and personal opinion from words and images to support understanding of evaluation within non-fiction.

Background knowledge

This section shows the children that non-fiction is not made up solely of literal facts. It explains how, whenever the author of a newspaper or magazine article writes about the ideas or feelings, thoughts, behaviours and motives of any individuals, groups or organisations, it is possible to have evaluation. Evaluation is often used in non-fiction writing to persuade and prompt emotional reaction.

Journalists are meant to provide an impartial view of the events or subject matter they are reporting on. However, their articles can be intentionally emotive and aim to influence the opinions of the readers. It is important therefore that the children are made aware of persuasion within non-fiction and that they feel able to distinguish fact from opinion in a report. To do this they need to draw on their prior knowledge, experience of life and common sense to help them recognise emotive language or exaggeration passed off as facts.

Skills

These activities help the children to learn how to distinguish the difference between literal facts and an author's personal opinion in non-fiction texts.

- **Photocopiable page 109 'Fact or fiction?'**
  - Explain that non-fiction is not always literal fact. Sometimes authors of newspaper or magazine articles use emotive language and exaggeration to persuade the reader or influence their opinion.

- Show the children a range of non-fiction articles from newspapers and magazines. Discuss how descriptive words and exaggeration are used to create a reaction in the reader. Show them how these reports differ from direct reporting that present plain information and figures with no description.
- Hand out the photocopiable sheet. Tell the children that they are required to use their evaluation skills, common sense and prior knowledge and experience of people and the world, to work out which are facts and opinion in the non-fiction text examples.
- Ask the children, working in groups, to read and discuss the contents of the page. Tell them to think about the purpose of the information. Ask: *Is it trying to persuade and alter opinion or is it simply informing you of data?* Ask them to underline any descriptive language or exaggerated claims to help them decide which reports are true or false.
- When the groups have agreed whether the information in each question is true or false, ask them to tick the appropriate box and write an explanation for their decision.

Comprehension

- **Photocopiable pages 110 and 111 'Lovely grub'**
  - Hand out the photocopiable sheets. Ask the children to read the text on the first sheet with a partner and discuss their opinions about it.
  - The children's personal experiences, knowledge and evidence from the text will be needed to support evaluative reasoning when answering the questions on the second sheet and generating their own questions from the information.

What's on the CD-ROM

On the CD-ROM you will find:
- Printable versions of all three photocopiable pages.
- Answers to 'Fact or fiction?' and 'Lovely grub (2)'.
- Interactive version of 'Fact or fiction?'.

Fact or fiction?

■ Underline the words that suggest whether the following texts are true or false.

1. Dogs are super-independent animals and are perfectly able to fend for themselves throughout the day. They do not need people's company or the companionship of other dogs. They behave badly and become appallingly spoilt if they are allowed to sleep and eat inside the house.

Fact ☐   Fiction ☐

Why do you think that? _____

_____

2. Hours spent watching TV has a negative effect on children's language because they spend little time in conversation with others. This makes it difficult for many of them to make friends.

Fact ☐   Fiction ☐

Why do you think that? _____

_____

3. British athletes are the most talented and highly trained in the world. They are on track to win a gold or silver medal in every category of the next Olympics.

Fact ☐   Fiction ☐

Why do you think that? _____

_____

4. The Moon travels around the Earth. It takes 28 days to go around this orbit. The Earth moves around the Sun; it takes 365 days (one year) to go all the way around. As the Earth moves around the Sun it is spinning. It takes 24 hours (one day) to spin around on its axis.

Fact ☐   Fiction ☐

Why do you think that? _____

_____

Illustration © 2009, JHS Studio/Beehive Illustration.

Name:

Fact, opinion and evaluation

Lovely grub (1)

In 2004 a UN report promoted the idea of eating insects.

Insects are a brilliant food source – simple to look after and easy to harvest. Many insects are high in protein and low in fats. Why don't we eat insects every day? Many people do eat insects as part of their regular diet. They eat sago grubs in Papua New Guinea. In Mexico people tuck into grasshoppers and in Bali dragonflies are popular. In America some fancy restaurants put dishes like stir-fried mealworms or caterpillar crunch on the menu.

Insects taste best if cooked when they're alive; or if they're very lively, freeze them first to slow them down. Larvae are often easier to eat than adult insects – no crunchy outside parts to get stuck in your teeth.

We really should all try sautéed caterpillar – they are delicious. Everyone would enjoy chocolate-dipped ants or, better still, juicy bees drizzled with white chocolate and honey.

Entomophagy (the correct term for insect eating) is the sensible way forward. Don't pick the little worm out of your apple – eat it, enjoy the taste and make use of that extra protein.

If you still feel squeamish about munching moth pupae or nibbling on crispy locusts or chilli-roast termites, then disguise them. Use a blender! Whiz them up in sauces and soups. Make fantastic high-protein smoothies – tell your friends after they've drunk them that it was a strawberry and wasp grub sensation or a banana bug detox that they just enjoyed!

Elspeth Graham

Lovely grub (2)

1. Was this article written simply to inform? What clues tell you this?

_____

_____

2. Do you think it is true that fancy American restaurants serve 'caterpillar crunch' on the menu? Explain why you say this.

_____

_____

3. Give an example of the author's attempt to shock the reader. Do you think she is successful? Explain why you think so.

_____

_____

4. Do you believe the author when she says that the UN (United Nations) promoted the idea of eating insects in 2004? What reason do you have for saying that?

_____

_____

5. Has the author persuaded you that eating insects would be good for you or enjoyable? Why do you say that?

_____

_____

6. Your evaluation question:

_____

_____

    Your answer:

_____

_____

Evaluation questions

To understand that evaluation questions ask you to use a mix of literal, inferred and personal understanding to answer them and to generate questions about characters' feelings or actions.

Background knowledge

Children need to understand that in order to answer and generate their own evaluation questions with well-reasoned responses, they need a combination of literal, inference and deduction skills – with the addition of their own understanding of the world. These skills help them to empathise with and understand the characters they are reading about. They must first locate the literal 'who', 'what' and 'where' information within the text and pictures, then search for inference word and picture clues that suggest the characters' feelings and points of view in the story. When they add their own experience and prior knowledge to the mix, it helps to guide them towards an explanation of the character's thoughts and actions.

Skills

This activity helps the children to draw on literal and inference skills plus personal experiences to ask questions and justify responses to evaluation questions from pictures and text.

- **Photocopiable page 113 'Characters' thoughts'**
  - Remind the children that in order to ask and answer evaluation questions, private detectives need to combine their literal and detective skills (see poster pages 27 and 63), as well as knowledge from their own experiences, to locate word and picture clues that suggest what the characters are thinking, how they feel and why they are behaving in a particular way.

- Remind the children that answers that are drawn from their own experiences also need to link to evidence in the text and pictures.
- Tell the children that this activity helps them to identify feelings and thoughts associated with anticipation and prior experience, and asks them to locate clues and make links to ask and answer evaluation questions.
- Hand out the photocopiable sheet and talk with the children about the 'who', 'what' and 'where' information within the picture and text.
- Ask them to imagine that they are the boy in the picture and poem. What do they think he is feeling, from the expression on his face and his body language?
- Tell the children to locate the words in the poem that link to the picture clues and that explain further what is happening and why.
- Ask the children to fill in the thought bubble, expressing what the boy is thinking, and to answer the questions at the foot of the sheet.

Comprehension

- **Photocopiable pages 114 and 115 'Chips'**
  - Hand out the photocopiable sheets. Ask the children to read the poem on the first sheet. You may find it appropriate to discuss healthy eating here and explain that chips are fine to have once in a while, but that the children need to ensure that they eat a balanced diet.
  - To answer the questions on the second sheet, ask the children to link the clues in each question with those in the picture and text that relate to the character's feelings. Then prompt them to ask and answer their own questions.

What's on the CD-ROM

On the CD-ROM you will find:
- Printable versions of all three photocopiable pages.
- Answers to 'Characters' thoughts' and 'Chips (2)'.
- Interactive version of 'Characters' thoughts'.

Characters' thoughts

■ Read the poem. What is the character feeling? Complete the thought bubble.

Facts about air

Scientists say
That air consists
Of about 78% nitrogen and
21% oxygen
Plus some carbon dioxide
And some amounts
Of the rare gases – helium, argon
and neon.

These are facts, I know.
But I also know
That when I go outside
On a spring morning
The air tastes as crisp
As a fresh lettuce
And that when I sit
On the patio
On a summer evening
The cool night air
Brushes my cheek like a feather.

John Foster

■ Now answer these questions on a separate piece of paper.

1. What do you think the character means by 'the air tastes as crisp as a fresh lettuce'? Why do you say that?

2. Explain why you think he said 'The cool night air brushes my cheek like a feather.'

3. How do you think the character is feeling? Why do you say that?

Name:

Chips (1)

■ What is the boy thinking? Complete the thought bubble.

Chips

Out of the paper bag
Comes the hot breath of the chips
And I shall blow on them
To stop them burning my lips.

Before I leave the counter
The woman shakes
Raindrops of vinegar on them
And salty snowflakes.

Outside the frosty pavements
Are slippery as a slide
But the chips and I
Are warm inside.

Stanley Cook

Chips (2)

1. How do you think the child in the poem is feeling? Explain why you say this.

_____

_____

_____

2. What do you think the child particularly likes about this food? Why do you say that?

_____

_____

3. Do you think the child feels comforted by chips? What clues tell you this?

_____

_____

4. Your evaluation question:

_____

_____

    Your answer:

_____

_____

5. Your evaluation question:

_____

_____

    Your answer:

_____

_____

Chapter 7

Review

Introduction

Instead of teaching children new skills, this chapter provides them with an opportunity to revise the skills they have already learned. There are four sections within the chapter. Each one provides a comprehension exercise that is levelled at a different reading age, between ages 7–11.

Poster notes

Follow my leader (page 117)

All of the posters in this book could be of use in this chapter, but especially this poster page. The poster reminds the children of the process involved in exploring a piece of text fully and provides a structure that enables them to consolidate everything they have learned. Working in teams, with a teacher as score master, the children score points for each question type they ask and answer from a piece of shared text. This is a useful way for them to establish questioning and answering techniques, to identify their own comprehension strengths and weaknesses, and to learn from each other.

In this chapter

	About the section	About the comprehension activity
Non-fiction page 118	This section focuses on the revision of the skills learned in the previous chapters for reading ages 7–9 years.	The first activity is based on a text with illustrations from *Making Faces* by Nick Butterworth, while the other focuses on an instructional text about making chunky chips.
Fiction page 123	This section focuses on the revision of the skills learned in the previous chapters for reading ages 9–11 years.	The first activity is based on an extract from Anthony Horowitz's *Stormbreaker*™ (a graphic novel) while the other is based on an extract from *Exchange* by Paul Magrs.

Review

Follow my leader

Predicting What happens next?		Use clues in titles, pictures, text and own experience to make predictions. Discuss predictions. Read text and look at the pictures.
Clarifying What does it mean?		Identify words and phrases you do not understand. Use context clues and picture clues to work out the meaning. Ask a teacher if you cannot work out the meaning.
Questioning What questions could I ask? Score: Literal: 1 Inference: 2 Evaluation: 3	 Who, what, where, when, why? Beginning, middle, end.	Ask questions: **who, what, where, why, how?** Ask and answer questions. You score points for good questions and correct answers. Discuss question type.
Retelling/summarising What have we read?		Summarise what you have read. Check you have covered the main points only. Change or add to the summary if necessary.
Predicting Choose another leader and repeat the cycle.		Predict what you think the next paragraph will be about (use last sentence, headings, pictures, own experiences). Discuss predictions.

Illustration © 2009, JHS Studio/Beehive Illustration.

Non-fiction

Objective

To identify the plot and sequence of events within picture stories and to gather clues and information from non-fiction pictures and text to answer questions.

Background knowledge

These two comprehension activities are aimed at children with a reading age of 7–9 years. The use of pictures for both texts sparks children's thinking on all levels and can inform as powerfully as words on a page. Pictures offer immediate information, but also invite deeper exploration to make greater sense of the images that link to text.

These activities focus on the skills the children have learned in the previous chapters that will enable them to gather the clues necessary to ask and answer questions.

It is important that children understand that non-fiction is about real things, people, events and places, and fiction is storytelling about imaginary people and events that do not exist. However, even though it is concerned with facts, it does not mean that non-fiction presents only literal information. There is plenty that can be inferred or evaluated from photographs and non-fiction text.

Comprehension

These activities will help the children search for clues to answer literal, inference and evaluation questions from pictures and text.

● **Photocopiable pages 119 and 120 'Making faces'**
This activity is levelled at a reading age of 7–8 years. Talk about the picture and vocabulary with the children before encouraging them to answer the literal, inference, evaluation and clarification questions from the picture and text. Each question type is awarded a mark:

- Question 1 is a literal question. (1 mark)
- Question 2 is a inference question. (2 marks)
- Question 3 is a literal question. (1 mark)
- Question 4 is an evaluation question. (3 marks)
- Question 5 is an evaluation question. (3 marks)

● **Photocopiable pages 121 and 122 'Chunky chips'**
This activity is levelled at a reading age of 8–9 years. Look at the photographs and instructions with the children before they tackle the questions. Each question type is awarded a mark:

- Question 1 is a literal question. (1 mark)
- Question 2 is a clarification question. (2 marks)
- Question 3 is an inference question. (2 marks)
- Question 4 is an inference question. (2 marks)
- Question 5 is an evaluation question. (3 marks)
- Question 6 is a clarification question. (3 marks)

What's on the CD-ROM

On the CD-ROM you will find:
- Printable versions of all four photocopiable pages.
- Answers to 'Making faces (2)' and 'Chunky chips (2)'.
- Interactive version of 'Making faces'.

Making faces (1)

Faces, Faces, Faces

Wherever you look you see faces.
People's faces. Animal faces.

Even cars seem to have faces.

The moon has a face. Clocks have faces.
And if you look carefully, you can see faces in
the clouds or in the shapes made by a fire.

Text and illustrations © 1993, Nick Butterworth.

Name:

Non-fiction

Making faces (2)

1. Who is the odd one out in the top picture?

_____

_____

(1 mark)

2. Is it possible to see faces up in the sky? How do you know that?

_____

_____

_____

(2 marks)

3. Where else can you see faces if you look carefully?

_____

_____

(1 mark)

4. Do you think the information on the page suggests that cars seem almost human? Why do you say that?

_____

_____

_____

_____

(3 marks)

5. Explain why you think clocks are described as having 'faces.'

_____

_____

_____

(3 mark)

Non-fiction

Chunky chips (1)

You will need
Small kitchen brush
Chopping board • Sharp knife
Small bowl • Pastry brush
Baking sheet

Ingredients
450 g (1 lb) potatoes
4–5 tablespoons sunflower
or olive oil
Salt and pepper

Tasty tips
To give a Mediterranean
flavour to the chips, sprinkle
them with dried mixed herbs
before cooking them.
Make delicious parsnip chips by
cooking parsnips in the same
way as potatoes.

Set the oven. Scrub the potatoes until clean. Cut them in half lengthwise, then cut them into narrow wedges.

Brush the baking sheet with oil. Lay the potato wedges in one layer on top, then brush them with oil and *season*.

Bake the potato wedges on the top shelf of the oven for about 20 minutes or until crisp, golden brown and puffy.

Chunky chips go well with many dishes and make a tasty snack on their own.

Tomato ketchup   *Mayonnaise for dipping*

Text © 1997, Angela Wilkes; photographs © 1997, Dorling Kindersley.

Name:

Chunky chips (2)

1. What ingredients do you need to make chunky chips?

    _____

    (1 mark)

2. Explain what 'season' means here.

    _____

    (2 marks)

3. Do you have to chop the potatoes up to make chips? How do you know that?

    _____

    _____

    (2 marks)

4. Does it take longer than an hour to cook the potatoes? How you know that?

    _____

    _____

    (2 marks)

5. Do you think the instructions for this recipe are helpful? Explain why you say that.

    _____

    _____

    _____

    (3 marks)

6. How do you think you could use this recipe to produce different flavoured chips?

    _____

    _____

    _____

    (3 mark)

Fiction

Objectives

To skim and scan for literal, inferential and evaluative information. To respond to questions by locating the same, similar or opposite meanings to key words in the questions and generate questions.

Background knowledge

These two comprehension activities are aimed at children with a reading age of 9–11 years. The questioner is testing the reader's understanding of vocabulary within context. He also wants to see if the reader understands what the key words in the question actually mean. It is important that children understand that key words in questions are linked in their meaning to clue words in the text and information within the pictures, and that they simply need to search for similar or opposite word meanings to find the answers to the questions. These activities enable them to practise their skimming and scanning techniques to help them find the clue words in text with speed and accuracy.

Comprehension

These activities will remind the children how to understand unknown words from context and how to skim and scan for information to help them answer questions.

● **Photocopiable pages 124 and 125 'Stormbreaker™'**

This activity is levelled at a reading age of 9–10 years. Ask the children to search the pictures and text for clues to answer literal, inference, clarification, evaluation and prediction questions. Each question type is awarded a mark:

- Question 1 is a literal question. (1 mark)
- Question 2 is a clarification question. (2 marks)
- Question 3 is an inference question. (2 marks)
- Question 4 is a prediction question. (2 marks)
- Question 5 is an evaluation question. (3 marks)

● **Photocopiable pages 126 and 127 'Exchange'**

This final comprehension activity is levelled at a reading age of 10–11 years. It asks the children to skim and scan the text for same and similar meanings to find the answers to a range of questions. Each question type is awarded a mark:

- Question 1 is a literal question. (1 mark)
- Question 2 is a clarification question. (2 marks)
- Question 3 is an inference question. (2 marks)
- Question 4 is an evaluation question. (3 marks)
- Question 5 is an evaluation question. (3 marks)
- Question 6 is an prediction question. (2 marks)

What's on the CD-ROM

On the CD-ROM you will find:
- Printable versions of all four photocopiable pages.
- Answers to 'Stormbreaker™ (2)' and 'Exchange (2)'.
- Interactive version of 'Exchange'.

Stormbreaker™ (1)

Text and illustrations © 2006, Walker Books Ltd.

Fiction

Stormbreaker™ (2)

1. What can be fired from a range of six metres?

    _____

    (1 mark)

2. Explain what you think the man means by 'bug-finder.'

    _____

    _____

    _____

    (2 marks)

3. Is the boy able to contact the man with the PDA scanner? How do you know that?

    _____

    _____

    _____

    (2 marks)

4. What do you predict they are getting ready to do? What clues tell you this?

    _____

    _____

    _____

    (2 marks)

5. What do you think might be the most useful gadget out of all the devices given to the boy? Explain why you say that.

    _____

    _____

    _____

    (3 marks)

Name:

Fiction

Exchange (1)

They started laughing as soon as they saw him. Simon could hear them from miles away, and he knew he would have to walk past. He would have to brave it out as they laughed their heads off. They'd be jeering and pointing at the tartan shopping bag he was pulling along behind him. It was on wheels and it belonged to his gran.

Why had he let her talk him into taking her shopping bag? Why hadn't he just used normal carrier bags from the supermarket? Everyone else did. Only old pensioners used shopping bags on wheels to fetch their groceries from the shops. Not sixteen-year-old lads. Not unless they were freaks. Freaks who let their grans talk them into using pensioners' bags and who got laughed at in the street by all the other kids.

Kids who don't even know me, he thought. I've only been in this town a couple of months. They don't know anything about me. What gives them the right to go yelling at me?

He knew, though. He knew what it was that gave them the right.

I'm an easy target, he thought.

Text © 2006, Paul Magrs; illustration © 2009, JHS Studio/Beehive Illustration.

SCHOLASTIC
www.scholastic.co.uk

Name:

Fiction

Exchange (2)

1. Who had talked Simon into taking the shopping bag?

_____

(1 mark)

2. What is meant by 'freaks' here?

_____

_____

(2 marks)

3. Was Simon new to the area? How do you know that?

_____

_____

(2 marks)

4. Do you think Simon was a caring teenager? Why do you say that?

_____

_____

_____

(3 marks)

5. Do you think Simon was lonely? Explain why you think this.

_____

_____

(3 marks)

6. Explain what you think happens next in this story.

_____

_____

_____

(2 marks)

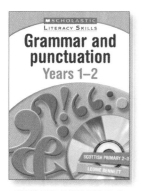
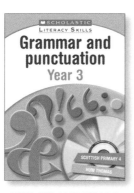
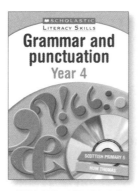
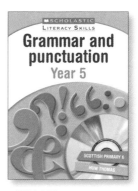
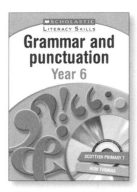

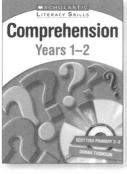
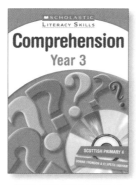
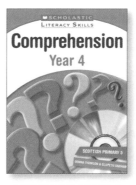
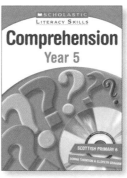
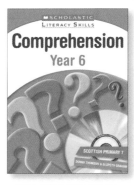

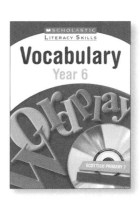